An Evaluation of the Intensity of

Radical Islam in the Balkans and the Assessment

of Its Level of Threat for European Security

A Monograph
by
MAJ Gjorgji Veljovski
Macedonian Army

MENS EST CLAVIS VICTORIAE

School of Advanced Military Studies
United States Army Command and General Staff College
Fort Leavenworth, Kansas

AY 2012-001

Abstract

AN EVALUATION OF THE INTENSITY OF RADICAL ISLAM IN THE BALKANS AND ASSESSMENT OF ITS LEVEL OF THREAT FOR EUROPEAN SECURITY by MAJ Gjorgji Veljovski, Macedonian army, 63 pages.

In the past two decades, Radical Islam rooted in Europe became an obvious security threat. This monograph argues that Western Europeans are partially responsible for permitting or not preventing the presence of radical Islamists in the Balkans and therefore in EU. While Islam came in Western Europe with the wave of immigration from African and Asian Muslim countries in the 1970s and 1980s, Islam in the Balkans existed for centuries. Radical Islam in Europe was initially imported from the mujahedeens that came to fight in the Balkan wars in the 1990s, and only later boosted by the events of the post 9/11 world.

To define a valid problem statement, this monograph offers understanding of the cultural differences between the Western European Muslims and the Balkan Muslims. While the Balkan Muslims that lived on European soil for centuries are among the most secular in the world, Western European Muslims that are recent immigrants are showing high level of intolerance and radicalism, opposing the democratic values embedded in Western European culture. The Western European states failed to integrate Muslims into their societies and declared the idea of multiculturalism as a failed project, at the same time asking the Balkans governments to accommodate Muslims, indirectly facilitating the infiltration of radical Islam.

The purpose of this monograph is to evaluate the intensity of radical Islam in the Balkans compared with the same problem that Western Europe has, by explaining the connections between Balkans Islam and Western European Islam. The patterns show that radical Islamists' strategic objective is Western Europe, and not the Balkans itself. Balkan countries are merely a safe haven for radical Islam and base for further operations into Western Europe.

The Muslim population in several Balkan states is vulnerable to the emergence of radical Islam that in the past two decades is targeting moderate Muslims using the social-economic instability in the Balkans and support from the global jihadist network. This monograph suggests that Western European countries must establish a joint and decisive strategic concept for preventing radicalization of its Muslim population, not excluding the Balkan countries as a significant factor for the overall European security.

Table of Contents

CHAPTER 1
INTRODUCTION

In the end, Europe's enemy is not Islam, or even radical Islam. Europe's enemy is itself - its self-destructive passivity, its softness toward tyranny . . .[1]

It is obvious that after the end of the Cold War, the political and cultural tension grew between the Muslim world and the West (United States and Europe).[2] Especially after the conflicts in Afghanistan, Iraq, Iran, Chechnya, Bosnia, Kosovo, and attacks in Tanzania and Kenya, "Islamic culture came to be regarded as incompatible with Western values and perceived as a major political threat to the West."[3]

The radical Islamists were acting globally for years, but not until the biggest terrorist attack ever on 9/11, was this movement recognized as a global transnational phenomenon and a threat that must be addressed more seriously. It turned out that in the aftermath of the 9/11 attacks, different Islamic groups, although from different nationalities with different agendas, some even hostile to one another, united and celebrated the attacks against the biggest country of the Western World. This reaction woke up Europe as well, and it was dawning on European leaders that the radical Islamists had a homogenous ideology and probably similar objectives.

Some authors portray the 9/11 hijackers and other Muslim terrorists as a product of Westernization of Islam because they spent time in the West, allegedly ignored, isolated, and

---

[1] Bruce Bawer, *While Europe Slept: How Radical Islam is Destroying the West from Within* (New York: Broadway books, 2006), 233.

[2] Bryan Turner, "Orientalism and otherness" in *Islam in the European Union, Transnationalism, Youth and the War on Terror*, ed. Yunas Samad and Kasturi Sen (Oxford University Press 2007), 68.

[3] Ibid., 69.

somehow oppressed by their hosts.[4] However, almost all of them were born and raised in the Muslim world and came to the West with an eastern idea of the Islamic community (Umma). Ultimately, they were a product of the Muslim fundamentalism that was originally aimed against their own secular governments. However, the West never directly threatened their way of life in the Muslim World.

The subject of this monograph is the threat of radical Islam in the Balkans, and how this affects the rest of Europe. It seems that Western European leaders have erased the Balkans from the memory of European decision makers. Hundreds of years ago, they considered the Mediterranean Sea as a natural border between Europe and the Muslims. After the Ottoman conquest of the Balkans and failed siege of Vienna, they considered the Balkans as a new border between their states and Islam and thus a lost cause for development. Today, even a moderate German Muslim, Professor Bassam Tibi, who advocates "Euro Islam" among the Muslims, barely mentions the word "Balkans" - as the Balkan Muslims are not within Europe in his mind, and they do not need to accept the concept of "Euro Islam," although they comprise roughly one third of the European Muslim population. West Europeans are in denial that Balkan security is not crucial for overall European security, and in the contemporary environment, this allows for the emergence of radical Islam.

Ethno - religious war, nationalism, collapsed economies, organized crime, and unstable governments, made the Balkans vulnerable to the expansion of radical Islam in the past two decades. While Western Europe is becoming stricter with its Islamic population, it encourages a multicultural posture on the Balkans and pressures Balkan states to show greater tolerance toward

---

[4] Alison Pargeter, *The New Frontiers of Jihad - Radical Islam in Europe* (Philadelphia: University of Pennsylvania Press, 2008), 110.

Islam. While they are aware of the danger of the radical Islam in their countries, they suggest Balkan governments make compromises with their own indigenous Islamic populations. It is obvious that interest about the spreading of radical Islam in Europe is focused on the Western Europe, not on the Balkans. Some believe it should be exactly the opposite. This monograph will examine both sides and justify or refute the Western European posture.

The Research Question

Although ethnic groups in the Balkans primarily identified themselves through religion, post-communist nationalism motivated the Yugoslav wars (1991 - 2001). Muslims fought Christians, but also Christians fought other Christians (Serbs and Croats), which does not entirely comply with Huntington's theory on the clash of civilizations. However, it is undeniable that the Muslim world clearly perceived the Yugoslav wars as Islam in peril, and rushed to help by any means necessary. What was left after the war were pockets of indoctrinated Imams and fundamentalists that, after the radical Islamists called for global jihad, became a serious security threat.

Today the emergence of radical Islam seems to be a number one concern in Europe, especially after attacks in Europe in a post 9/11 world. Although Muslim fundamentalism spurred from the West European Muslim ghettoes after the end of the Cold War, many believe that the Balkan wars have facilitated the infiltration of radical Islam onto European soil. In the past two decades, the presence of Mujahedeen veterans and many Islamic charity organizations in the Balkans created many concerns among Europeans.

However, the Balkan Muslims are among the most secular in the world, which raises the question whether there is a genuine threat for the European security from the emergence of radical Islam in the Balkans or if it is an exaggerated fear by Balkan states seeking to exploit a latent fear following the trends of the global war on terror? The thinking postulated above leads to the following hypotheses that will be examined in this paper:

Hypothesis 1: The Western European states failed to integrate Muslims into their societies and declared the idea of multiculturalism as a failed project, at the same time pressuring some of the Balkans governments to accept the multicultural idea and accommodate Muslims, indirectly facilitating the infiltration of radical Islam.

Hypothesis 2: The Muslim population in several Balkan states is vulnerable to the emergence of radical Islam that in the past two decades is targeting moderate Muslims using the social-economic instability in the Balkans and support from the global jihadist network.

Hypothesis 3: Radical Islam's strategic objective is Western Europe, and not the Balkans itself, which is becoming merely a safe haven for terrorism and base for further operations into Western Europe. It seems that in the past two decades the Europeans ignored the threat of radical Islam entering to EU through the Balkans, leaving the Balkan states to fight alone.

Historical Background

Besides rejecting Balkan Muslims from European soil, another phenomenon is present after the Yugoslav Wars (1991 - 2001). This is overemphasis, misuse, and violation of the concept of multiculturalism, which Western Europe projected on the Balkans in an attempt to secure permanent peace. Accidently, this policy opened the doors to radical Islam in the past two decades by supporting the establishment of Muslim states in the heart of Europe.

The West turned blind eye during the Yugoslav wars, when thousands of mujahedeen fighters came to the Balkans to propagate global jihad, which started in the first Afghan war. They also ignored the activities of dozens of Islamic organizations that helped jihadists and triggered Wahhabi style Islam, until then unknown to the secular Balkan Muslims. Radical Islamists perceived the Balkans as the weak spot for infiltration and a major weakness of Western Europe.

It is important to clearly identify if there is a real problem with Islam in the Balkans. So far, many biased authors and officials failed to make a distinction between political Islam,

4

fundamentalism, and radical Islam, and many portray all Balkan Muslims as a potential security threat. These claims can compromise future Balkan integration into the European Union (EU.) It would be the same policy of failed integration that the West Europeans just recently admitted.

The radical Islamists prey on the moderate Muslims first by establishing a fundamentalist environment. If the Balkans governments do not support moderate, secular Muslims to reject Islamic fundamentalism, they might be pushed toward radicalism. The Muslims themselves, with necessary help by the Balkan governments, must confront radical Islam. That is why it is crucial to define the real problem and address it by offering policies to stop the radical threat by integrating Muslims into the European culture.

Although the Balkans is not viewed by Western experts as a serious threat and a key region for breeding Islamists' terrorism,[5] its continuing problems are still making the region vulnerable for recruitment of potential radicals. From the viewpoint of the radical Islamists, the Balkans became a safe haven with a well - established Muslim infrastructure connected to the broader Muslim world. The Bosnian war and the involvement of the Muslim jihad opened a new chapter in European security policy, bringing radical Islam closer to Western Europe.

However, compared with Western Europe, the Balkans, while suspected to be more vulnerable to radical Islam because of the lower economic development, is actually less attractive to immigrants from the Muslim World, making the potential recruitment pool smaller than the one in Western European countries.[6] According to Bougarel, "it would be unjustified and dangerous to present Balkan Islam and its current evolutions as a threat to Europe . . . the Muslim

---

[5] Steven Woehrel, "Islamic Terrorism and the Balkans," (CRS Report for Congress, July 26, 2005).

[6] Ibid.

5

populations of this region are not a crisis factor, but victims and actors among others in a wider regional crisis."[7] At the same time, the burden of responsibility to compel radical Islamists is in their hands, because their integration into Europe will be compromised if they are identified as using Islam to achieve political goals.[8]

The final assumption is that the Balkan governments often are motivated to hunt terrorists as a method of seeking political support from the United States by portraying the Balkan region as marked as a potential source of terrorism.[9] The positive thing from these policies is that the constant alert and awareness for terrorism is actually helpful in the global picture, making the states cooperate more in the field of security. A potential negative consequence is losing the most important ally in confronting radical Islam in the Balkans - the Muslim population.

---

[7] Xavier Bougarel, "Islam and politics in the post - communist Balkans" (paper presented for the Socrates Kokkalis Student Workshop : New Approaches to Southeast Europe, Cambridge, February 12-13, 1999), 17.

[8] Ibid., 17.

[9] Steven Woehrel, "Islamic Terrorism and the Balkans," (CRS Report for Congress, July 26, 2005).

CHAPTER 2
LITERATURE REVIEW

It seems that in the contemporary security environment, globalization facilitated the rise of terrorism and unified religious fanatics in their irrational cause. Throughout history, religious disagreements killed more people than any other reason. While it provided people with comfort and hope, it also provided justification for violence. Mark Juergensmeyer's *Terror in the Mind of God* examines how cultures and religions fit in the context of terrorism. However, religion and culture most of the time are not a reason for violence itself, but only tools used by extremists to justify their political objectives and recruit members. In many cases, the violence in conflicts will eventually seek religious validation.[10]

Islam is not necessarily connected with violence, but radical Islamists found support in Islam to justify their struggle as "holy." They use fundamentalists' ideas to support their political agenda, presenting it in pure religious context. In Europe, radical Islam had become a security threat in the past two decades. There is much literature written on the subject of radical Islam in Europe and the Balkans. When authors write about Europe, often they think of EU, or only Western Europe as it was during the Cold War, without the new member states from the former Eastern Europe. Nevertheless, almost all quietly agree that there is a significant cultural difference between European Muslims, which are "new Muslims," or immigrants from the Muslim world, and Balkan Muslims, which are "old Muslims," or old European citizens converted in Islam centuries ago.

While some authors offer much evidence that the Balkans is a breeding ground for radical

---

[10] Mark Juergensmeyer, *Terror in the Mind of God: the Global Rise of Religious Violence* (Los Angeles: University of California Press, 2000), 161.

Islam, portraying the Balkan Muslim community as a time bomb, there are many arguments that in fact, the situation is far from terrible and it is not a serious threat to future European security. The Balkan Muslims are moderate, secular, and less attracted to fundamentalism (as a first step to radicalism) than the Western European Muslims. For many authors, if Western European Muslims are compared with centuries old Balkan Muslims, although considered third generations Europeans, they are still very fresh and thus culturally not compatible with Europeans.

The literature goes from one side of the spectrum to the other. From the all - black scenarios of the centuries old argument of Muslim conquest of Europe, to the optimistic future of multiculturism and coexistence of cultures where radical Islam will be rejected by the very Muslim population in Europe. It is a challenge to find unbiased opinion and realistic assessment if the lines of operations of the radical Islamists are coming from the Balkans; they are directly accessing West Europe, or both.

Evan Kohlmann in *Al-Qaida's Jihad in Europe - the Afghan-Bosnian Network* provides historical evidence about the infiltration of radical Islam in the Balkans during the Bosnian war. He claims that the role of mujahedeen fighters in the Bosnian war was a continuance of global jihad that started in the Afghan war against the Soviets. The connections between mujahedeen fighters in the Balkans with Islamic terror organizations are well documented, culminating with undeniable proof that Al Qaeda supported the war effort of the jihadists in the Balkans.

Kohlmann's work supports this monograph in several ways. Although some mujahedeen came to Bosnia because they were denied return in their home countries, many consciously came to fight a holy war. They all used Islamic humanitarian aid and charities intended for civilians provided by many Muslim countries. These sponsors that rejected their return home after the Afghan war, at the same time facilitated their jihad, indirectly by providing military aid intended for the Bosnian army. Further, the Bosnian government that officially invited them to fight, legitimized their presence after the war by granting them citizenship. At the same time, UN forces in Bosnia, and Western European policymakers knew about their presence and did not see that as

8

possible future problem.

This is important to support the hypotheses that Western Europe unintentionally opened the doors to the radical Islam in the Balkans in the 1990s and it should be held responsible to help the Balkan governments closing them. It is a sensitive subject because the role of EU in the recent Balkan wars was confusing in a way that provided questionable short-term solutions for fast peace on the Balkans without envisioning the strategic future of Europe in terms of the rise of political Islam and its violent form, the global jihad.

Shaul Shay, *Islamic Terror and the Balkans* and Christopher Deliso *The Coming Balkan Caliphate - The Threat of radical Islam to Europe and the West* are describing the Balkans in the worst possible way, vulnerable to radical Islam and a time bomb for European security. Both of them use a very biased approach, underestimating the traditional practice of Muslim religion among the Balkan Muslims, which is compatible, and in fact culturally not much different from non-Muslim Balkan nations. They are viewing the Yugoslav wars as a religious struggle, not as nationalistic with the purpose of nation-building. The most false thesis is their claim that Bosnians and Albanians had religious motives to wage war, a claim that they support with questionable sources. In their works, they used already biased opinions and sources, for example Serbian intelligence, which portrays all Balkan Muslims in an unacceptable way.

These authors support the theory of a "green axis" of Muslim expansion to Europe coming through the Balkans from the Arab World. They openly blame the Muslim charities and humanitarian organizations to be involved in, or support terror activities. Sources from these books must be double - checked for reliance, biases, and prejudice. Still, they are useful as they give historic description of events, some well-known facts, and review many involved actors that may be responsible for the attempt to radicalize the Balkans. Moreover, they offer strong arguments that Western Europe should not ignore Radical Islamism's efforts in the Balkans.

One of the solutions regarding how to peacefully accommodate Islam in European democratic culture is offered by Bassam Tibi through developing a so-called Euro-Islam. In

9

Political Islam, World Politics, and Europe - Democratic Peace and Euro-Islam versus Global jihad, he suggests that Muslims must bridge their religious beliefs with Western ideals by accepting the democratic values and political culture that already exists in Europe. Many believe that the nature of Islam is not compatible with democracy. Tibi agrees that there is a pattern of divergence in Europe but claims that it is not inevitable clash of cultures, and if European Muslims try to adapt to European culture, they can be accepted by the Europeans and not viewed as foreigners any more. Such accommodation of Muslims in Europe must be religious, political, and cultural at the same time, and can never be achieved forcefully. It is a dilemma between the Muslims in Europe, or as Tibi says, between "those Muslims who embrace democracy as a political culture and others who adhere to Islamism as a totalitarian ideology."[11]

Euro-Islam ought to be open, tolerant, and peaceful, and able to coexist with other religions. Because Tibi does not talk about Balkan Muslims at all, it is obvious that Balkan Islam already achieved these qualities. This is used in the monograph as an argument that native Balkan Muslims are more moderate, secular and European oriented than the immigrant Western European Muslims, thus less vulnerable to cross to the "dark side" of Islam.

The various literatures about Islam in Europe often connect the emergence of political Islam with the radical Islam. It is a trap that ought to be avoided by applying careful selection of sources. Surprisingly, many authors do not distinguish those and additionally fuel the complex Islamic problem in Europe. In general, the monograph will use as many sources as possible to offer an unbiased, realistic analysis and produce conclusions and recommendations, which will be valid and useful when thinking about the role of Balkans in the European security.

---

[11] Bassam Tibi, *Political Islam, World Politics and Europe - Democratic Peace and Euro - Islam Versus Global Jihad* (New York: Routledge, 2008), xii.

CHAPTER 3
METHODOLOGY

The first part of the analysis describes the origins of European Islam, rooted in the wave of immigration from African and Asian Muslim countries in the 1970s and 1980s. Further, it is important to explain why second and third generation Muslims in Western Europe became attracted to radical Islam after the end of the Cold War. The key to explaining this pattern is through the Islamic jihad developed in the Afghan war (1979 - 1989) that entered European soil in the Balkans during the Bosnian war (1992 - 1995). The second part of the analysis explains mujahedeen infiltration in Bosnia and the level of influence they made to the traditional Balkan Islam.

Using the comparative method, the monograph offers a better understanding of the cultural differences between the Western European Muslims and the Balkan Muslims, necessary to clarify which mindset is more vulnerable, first to Islamic fundamentalism, and second to Islamic terrorism. With the secular past of the Balkan Muslims on one side, and returning to the roots - mentality for the European Muslims on the other, produces different outputs when radical groups try to a establish stronghold among these Western Muslim communities.

Observation, supported by historical facts and analysis of current trends are the main methods used to evaluate the vulnerability of the Muslim population in the Balkans and Western Europe, juxtaposed against radical Islamists attempting to infiltrate these communities. The monograph covers a diverse range of authors and viewpoints on the subject in order to gain a fuller understanding of the situation. With many facts available, deductive reasoning should present a realistic image of the reality, which often is misrepresented to serve national policies.

The problem posed by the contemporary Islamic radical movement is a global one and cannot be understood fully solely in a regional or state analysis. Avoiding reductionism as a method when observing radical Islam is necessary to grasp the big picture. While on the micro-level reductionism is useful, in the case of this monograph and any other work on the subject of

Islam, it leads to only a partial understanding of the problem. Details cannot be ignored and reductionism could lead to inconclusive analysis and solutions that either do not solve anything or often, generate new problems.

This monograph covers all aspects and views, from biased Islamophobia and an irrational fear of Islam, to the reality of emergence of Islamic terror based on the attacks in Europe after 9/11. The retrospective of Yugoslavia will prove that the conflicts in this region were not religious in nature, but driven primarily from the struggle for national identity. However, it is a fact the radical Muslims - jihadists who came to participate in the Yugoslav wars had their own agenda. Most important, they are still present in the Balkans, with verified proof of involvement in radical networks connected to the events of 9/11.

Finally, the monograph will include an analysis of the implications for operational art, especially joint operations between European and Balkan militaries, which arise from the differing, and sometimes opposing, views of radical Islam in these regions. There is not a single European mind to enforce joint security policy. The biggest challenge will be to determine not just the unified European end-state for the problem of Radical Islam, but also the European end-state for the Balkans security in general.

Scope

This thesis will cover the period from the recent Yugoslav wars until today. It is necessary to cover the history of Islam in Europe and the characteristics of European and Balkan Islam. However, radical Islam is a relatively new phenomenon that is seemingly only taken seriously after the 9/11 attacks.

The Balkans has been home to Muslims for five centuries, since the Ottoman occupation. On the other hand, Western European countries have experience with the issues of Islam only in the past four decades, because of labor migration. The main difference is that the Balkan Muslims have always been de facto European citizens that converted to Islam centuries ago, while

European Muslims originate from Africa and Asia and may not yet have assimilated.

This monograph will cover several actors that have diametrically opposed strategies and agendas considering radical Islam. The EU and European Muslims, and Balkans states and Balkans Muslims are the targeted audience by Radical Islamists. Muslim countries supporting European Muslims through humanitarian aid and charity organizations, Muslim radicals with their militant networks, and terrorist organizations influence, facilitate, or directly support the growth of Radical Islam on European soil.

Limitations

There are more than enough books on Islam in Europe, but not many on the Balkans issue. Some explanation is that westerners do not want to write about the Balkan Islamic challenge because it is their fault. Others do not wish to wake the demons from the past Yugoslav wars. Either way, those who write are way too critical and biased in exaggerating that the Balkans is a nest of Radical Islam.

The biases are obvious, but used in the monograph to make a point that false assumptions will lead to false problem statements and, further, false solutions. In this monograph, all aspects will be covered, from one side of the spectrum to the other and the only limitation will be to minimize the opinions from the Balkans' authors. Naturally, they would the most biased describing the radical Islam in the Balkans. Most of the rest of the sources will be external, looking at the problem from the wider European perspective.

Significance of the Study

Radical Islam will continuously challenge Europe through the Balkans. It is geographically and demographically irresistible for the militant Islamists, additionally because there are many well - established Islamic organizations and infrastructure to support their activities. Even if there is not direct threat for the Balkans states, this study is significant because the real target is Western Europe.

The Balkan Muslim population is vulnerable and needs protection and support from all Balkan states, and EU. Western Europeans tried to enforce the model of Euro - Islam among their Muslim citizens, which is in fact, the model of a secular Balkan Islam. So called Euro-Islam has existed a long time in the Balkans and should be used as a model for European integration. However, Europeans somehow misuse the term "balkanization" to describe islamization which is a false assumption.

The significance of this thesis is to show how great the threat of radicalization is in the Balkans, compared with Western Europe, and to examine whether the EU should use Balkan methods of integration or vice versa. The results should offer suggestions and conclusions for practical use when we think about the infiltration of Radical Islam in the context of Euro - Balkans relations.

CHAPTER 4
ANALYSIS

Islam in Europe

Islam is the second largest religion in the EU. Today, around 20 million Muslims permanently live in Europe.[12] It all started when Western Europeans had to solve the problem of an increased need for labor in the 1970s and 1980s accepting any immigrants willing to work.[13] European countries had open door policies for immigrants that brought in millions of Muslim immigrants. They came primarily from the former European colonies (that spoke the European languages). They poured in to fill the labor gap, becoming an important part of the Western European economic boom, at first as a labor force, but later also as political refugees.[14]

Although Europeans thought the waves of Muslim immigrants would be a temporary labor solution, they began to settle permanently in Europe. Despite practicing Islam in the newly built mosques, second generation Muslims born in Europe started to attend European schools and accept European culture.[15] In the 1980s, Muslims in Europe started to actively participate in political and social life, and Muslim communities encouraged this trend.[16] Western Europeans chose fundamentally different approaches in their immigration policies from that of the United States, facilitating the trend of

---

[12] Bassam Tibi, *Political Islam, World Politics and Europe - Democratic Peace and Euro - Islam Versus Global Jihad* (New York: Routledge, 2008), 13.

[13] Konrad Pedziwiatr, "Muslims in Europe: Demography and organizations" in *Islam in the European Union, Transnationalism, Youth and the War on Terror*, ed. Yunas Samad and Kasturi Sen, (Oxford University Press 2007), 56.

[14] Ibid., 26.

[15] Samir Amghar, Amel Boubekeur and Michael Emerson, *European Islam Challenges for Public Policy and Society*, ed. Samir Amghar, Amel Boubekeur, and Michael Emerson (Brussels: Centre for European policy studies, 2007), 2.

[16] Ibid., 3.

integration. Instead of enforcing citizenship loyalties and assimilation in the state's culture, European political leaders agreed to promote a multicultural approach and accepted the cultural package that immigrants brought.[17] Western Europe tried to integrate its Muslim immigrants by embracing multicultural diversities, which turned out to be empty rhetoric years after this policy was initiated.[18]

Still, many authors offer misleading claims that the Muslim immigrants in Europe came from their countries simply to oppose Western way of life. Many Muslim immigrants left their homes as political refugees because they did not agree with the fact that citizens and sometimes the government forced traditional Islam and Sharia law. Political Islam in Europe was founded by "young idealists who were product of the internal social and political upheavals of their own societies and who had become involved in political Islam as a means of challenging their own governments."[19] The young Muslims that came to Europe in the 1980s were against traditional Islam and attracted to a fundamental version of Islam like Saudi Arabia's form of Wahhabism. Only later, radical Islamists will use them as a core for building networks in Europe.

The first sign of incompatibility of Islam and Europe took place after the Islamic revolution in Iran in 1979. The establishment of an Islamic state over the pro-Western monarchy had impact among all Muslims including the European immigrants. Until this event, different Muslim groups in Europe organized themselves based on their origin, ethnicity, and language. The Iranian revolution of 1979 initiated the idea of Muslim unity becoming a "symbol of hope and of resistance against imperialist

---

[17] Bruce Bawer, *While Europe Slept: How Radical Islam is Destroying the West from Within* (New York: Broadway books, 2006), 55.

[18] Ibid., 3.

[19] Alison Pargeter, *The New Frontiers of Jihad - Radical Islam in Europe* (Philadelphia: University of Pennsylvania Press, 2008), 6.

backed oppression."[20] Many European Muslims started to travel to Iran for education, as it opened its door of its religious institutes as an opportunity to project the Islamic theocracy and encourage Muslims to seek Umma.[21]

At the same time as the Iranian revolution, the Soviet invasion in Afghanistan triggered the emergence of jihad and Mujahedeen fighters, mainly supported by Saudi Arabia. The 1980s became a time of a rivalry between Saudi Arabia's Wahhabi version of Islam and Iran's Shia. Saudi Arabia started to promote and support Islam everywhere, including Europe, creating networks of charitable organizations.[22] Similar to Iran, Saudi Arabia invited students from all over the world to visit the country and receive free education, learning about the true version of Islam - Wahhabi.[23] Both countries were investing to project their ideology; however, the number one target group became the Muslim population in Western Europe, which was ethnically divided and vulnerable to westernization, on the path toward losing its identity as Muslims. The European continent became a sphere of interest for the Muslim world, and since the end of the Cold war, the players outside Europe influenced the change in Islamic behavior in Europe.[24] By the 1990s, Saudis dominated over Iranians and entirely trained and influenced the leadership of Muslim communities in Western Europe.[25]

However, the real problem with European Islam started after the end of the Soviet intervention in Afghanistan. Despite the glorious victory of Islam over the infidel superpower, many Muslim authorities

---

[20] Ibid., 17.

[21] Ibid., 18.

[22] Ibid., 21.

[23] Ibid., 21.

[24] "Islam in the European Union: What's at stake in the future?" (study requested by the European Parliament's committee on Culture and Education, Brussels, 14 May 2007), 15.

[25] Alison Pargeter, *The New Frontiers of Jihad - Radical Islam in Europe* (Philadelphia: University of Pennsylvania Press, 2008), 27.

did not allow the mujahedeen veterans to return home. Regimes in North Africa and the Middle East not only denied access to the mujahedeen; they even became more determined to clean their back yard from Islamists. Perceived as a possible security challenge, veterans were unwelcome to return to their countries.[26] Soon, waves of Muslims that were striving to return to their fundamental roots took refuge and had to seek shelter in West Europe running away from their governments.[27]

Apparently, convinced in the new earned power of Islam, the mujahedeen veterans' intention was ensuing action against regimes in their own countries, and the establishment of Islamic Arab World or the restoration of the old Caliphate.[28] Ironically, it was the Western way of life, values of freedom and democracy, which enabled the "newborn" radical Islamists to gain a strong foothold in Europe. At first, these political refugees did not intend to target Europe itself: "they viewed it as a useful and convenient place where they could set up Islamic centers and organizations and keep the flame of struggle burning in the lands of their birth."[29]

The Islamists took advantage of the European freedom of speech policy and started to build their propaganda network through various media.[30] London soon earned the nickname "Londonistan,"[31] becoming the number one European shelter for the radical Islamists. European security did not pay much attention to the fact that they were practically allowing insurgencies to undermine governments in the Arab World. Some of these were friendly to the Western World: "The freedom given to these individuals to disseminate propaganda and to rally for the cause among Muslim communities in Europe provoked

---

[26] Alison Pargeter, *The New Frontiers of Jihad - Radical Islam in Europe* (Philadelphia: University of Pennsylvania Press, 2008), 13.

[27] Ibid., 14.

[28] Ibid., 51.

[29] Ibid., 15.

[30] Ibid., 53.

[31] Ibid., 52.

much anger among the regimes of the Middle East."[32] Not only had they obtained asylum in Western Europe based on simply being unwelcome in their own countries, but they could reside freely anywhere and have social benefits.[33]

With the appearance of many Islamic groups in Europe, it was inevitable that they would start confronting each other. Europe turned out to be a battleground for the different Islamic groups, each promoting the true version of Islam.[34] For the first time the confrontation between jihadists spilled out of their sphere of interest in France, drawing the rest of Europe's attention in the mid - 1990s.[35] A radical group from Algeria sparked the existing unrest in the southern France, where a significant amount of Algerian Muslim immigrants lived since the end of colonialism. Slowly the Europeans would become targets to the radicals that firmly established their networks on European soil. The Arab-Afghan network continued with their jihad on European soil with intention of establishing a new base to export jihad outside the Muslim World.[36] Radical Islamists perceived Western European political correctness in tolerating Muslim intolerance as an infidel weakness.

On September 11, many young Muslims across Europe celebrated the terrorist actions of Al Qaeda in the streets.[37] The radical Islamists perceived European support to the United States as a

---

[32] Alison Pargeter, *The New Frontiers of Jihad - Radical Islam in Europe* (Philadelphia: University of Pennsylvania Press, 2008), 56.

[33] Bruce Bawer, *While Europe Slept: How Radical Islam is Destroying the West from Within* (New York: Broadway books, 2006), 225.

[34] Alison Pargeter, *The New Frontiers of Jihad - Radical Islam in Europe* (Philadelphia: University of Pennsylvania Press, 2008), 64.

[35] Ibid., 77.

[36] Evan Kohlmann, *Al - Qaida's Jihad in Europe - the Afghan - Bosnian Network* (New York, 2004), 30.

[37] Bruce Bawer, *While Europe Slept: How Radical Islam is Destroying the West from Within* (New York: Broadway books, 2006), 200.

provocation to attack European soil.[38] Soon after, radical Islamists started targeting Europe (Madrid on 11 March 2004, Amsterdam on 2 November 2004, and London in July 2005).[39] Obviously, radical Islamism in Europe managed to develop terror cells concealed among the Muslim communities that could be activated at any time. A well-organized series of attacks were undeniable proof that terrorist networks were already established and functioning on European soil years before.[40]

According to Leiken, there are two kinds of radical Muslims in Western Europe, "outsiders" and "insiders." The first are recent immigrants, refuges from the Muslim countries seeking asylum in Europe, like radical imams, "who open their mosques to terrorist recruiters and serve as messengers for or spiritual fathers to jihadist networks."[41] He claims that many of the outsiders deliberately migrated to Europe seeking jihad, because according to the Quran, migration is a form of Muslim conquest.[42] The second group, the insiders, is the second or third generation European born Muslims. Leiken claims that these groups of Muslims in Western Europe are the latest recruiters among the radical Islamists, acting as "the revolt of the second generation."[43] There is a pattern of a strategic and systematic attempt to recruit the third generation born insiders by Al Qaeda, especially after September 11 and United States operations in Iraq and Afghanistan.[44]

Although the United States considers herself as a primary modern target, the Islamists target

---

[38] Ibid., 154.

[39] Bassam Tibi, *Political Islam, World Politics and Europe - Democratic Peace and Euro - Islam Versus Global Jihad* (New York: Routledge, 2008), 4.

[40] "Islam in the European Union: What's at stake in the future?" (study requested by the European Parliament's committee on Culture and Education, Brussels, 14 May 2007), 29.

[41] Leiken, S. Robert, "Europe's Angry Muslims," *Foreign Affairs,* Vol. 84 Issue 4, (Jul/Aug 2005): 120-135.

[42] Ibid., 120-135.

[43] Ibid., 120-135.

[44] Ibid., 120-135.

Europe because they see Europeans as former crusaders,[45] holding them responsible for ending their Caliphate. In order to restore the Caliphate and create the new Islamic order, they intend to "de-Westernize the world at large within the framework of an Islamic system."[46] European countries have made themselves vulnerable through massive migration and developing the "belief that Islamic principles of order are universal."[47]

When the radical Islamists started to target Europe, many Western Europeans thought that the key for reconciliation were the "moderate" Muslims. One of the major policies of European countries is to isolate radical Islam by establishing support from the Muslim community.[48] Many Europeans constantly encouraged the "moderate" Muslims to step up and speak against radical Islam and growing fundamentalism among young Muslims. However, the truth is that the "moderate Muslim" is a Western concept, and some scholars argue there is no such thing as "moderate Muslim." Those Muslims that did not care that much about religion were still loyal to their culture. Bawer argues, "Many European Muslims may themselves be moderates, yet may have a concept of religious identity that makes it difficult for them to side with infidels against even the most violent of their fellow Muslims."[49]

After spending some time in West European cities, Bawer concluded that young European Muslims would always identify themselves first as Muslims loyal to their ancestral homeland. Bawer states, "Their neighborhoods aren't temporary ghettos that will fade away with integration, but embryonic

---

[45] Bassam Tibi, *Political Islam, World Politics and Europe - Democratic Peace and Euro - Islam Versus Global Jihad* (New York: Routledge, 2008), 4.

[46] Ibid., 16.

[47] Ibid., 16.

[48] Olivier Roy, "Islamic Terrorist Radicalization in Europe," in *European Islam Challenges for public policy and society*, ed. Samir Amghar, Amel Boubekeur, and Michael Emerson (Brussels: Centre for European policy studies, 2007), 57.

[49] Bruce Bawer, *While Europe Slept: How Radical Islam is Destroying the West from Within* (New York: Broadway books, 2006), 229.

colonies that will continue to grow as the result of immigration and reproduction."[50] Along with this, Western Europeans for decades could not accept the fact that Muslim immigrants view Islam more than just an expression of culture like the secular Christians in Europe do.[51] On one side, any attempt to enforce certain values that are compatible with European standards can inflame a reaction among Muslims that Europeans are islamophobic, and at the same time rejecting the European values inflames a reaction among Europeans that Muslims are not loyal and have a subversive ideology creating a vicious cycle of mistrust and enmity.

European countries are facing a set of challenges when merging the Islamic tradition with the pluralistic environment, in the attempt to fulfill minority rights and accommodate its Muslim population in the secularized democracy.[52] There is growing number of angry Imams in many European cities, encouraging the Muslim population to resist westernization and integration into society.[53] Their strategy is to oppose the European system by denouncing everything that is not in accordance with the Quran. By challenging the authorities in Europe, they are challenging the European determination and belief system, often using European tolerance in their speeches as proof of weakness and the corruption of morality of the Western ways.

In the past two decades, especially after 9/11, discrimination is one of the strongest reasons for

---

[50] Ibid., 32.

[51] Ibid., 34.

[52] Jocelyne Ceasari, "The Hybrid and Globalized Islam of Western Europe," in *Islam in the European Union, Transnationalism, Youth and the War on Terror*, ed. Yunas Samad and Kasturi Sen, (Oxford University Press, 2007), 109.

[53] Bassam Tibi, *Political Islam, World Politics and Europe - Democratic Peace and Euro - Islam Versus Global Jihad* (New York: Routledge, 2008), 22.

disaffection among the European Muslim community.[54] Such a trend is preventing integration of young Muslims, bringing disappointment, and feeding radicalization. However, the truth is that the majority of the European Muslims demand to be recognized as European citizens. Aware of the cultural context in Europe, the struggle for their European identity is important to them. A majority of the European Muslims do not see radical Islam as a way out, and at least, are very passive toward Islamism imported from outside of Europe. To support this statement, after European Imams called for protests after the global Muslim backlash against derogatory Danish cartoons of Mohamed, European Muslims did not protest in meaningful numbers.[55]

Having noted this, Pargeter reminds us that it is misleading to "disassociate the radicalism of the jihadists from their own roots . . . there is a cultural mindset that is present in the Islamic world that has proved prone to radicalism."[56] Fundamentalists that live in Europe, although a minority, still view Western civilization as corrupt and decadent.[57] There is a fair assumption that the idea of cultural incompatibility is more of a Muslim problem. Muslims that migrated in Europe do often isolate themselves in the ghettoes because they are the ones not tolerant toward the non-Muslims. Further proof that Muslim isolation comes from the fact that Europeans in the 1990s ignored the radicalization of Islam that would become a strategic challenge in the next century. Radical Muslims saw European tolerance as a weakness and turned against the very values that made their existence possible outside their home countries.

---

[54] Tufyal Choudhury, "Muslims and Discrimination," in *European Islam Challenges for Public Policy and Society*, ed. Samir Amghar, Amel Boubekeur, and Michael Emerson (Brussels: Centre for European policy studies, 2007), 77.

[55] Samir Amghar, Amel Boubekeur and Michael Emerson, *European Islam Challenges for Public Policy and Society* (Brussels: Centre for European policy studies, 2007), 5.

[56] Alison Pargeter, *The New Frontiers of Jihad - Radical Islam in Europe* (Philadelphia: University of Pennsylvania Press, 2008), 113.

[57] Ibid., 113.

In addition, Shay offers proof that the Islamic institutions in Europe are facilitating recruitment of new cadres for Islamic jihad, enticing young Muslims in Europe to "examine the path of a Global jihad as an ideological alternative to the Western secular culture."[58] It is not surprising that the second and third generations of European born Muslims are willing to choose that path. In multiethnic Europe, there is growing sentiment toward the emigrants' children as "foreigners who are sons of foreigners,"[59] especially in the contemporary environment of global terrorism and rise of global jihad in the past two decades. That makes the Islamic radicalism in Europe a youth movement.[60] Many authors still struggle to explain why this is happening. There are explanations like poverty, exclusion, racism, acculturation, which are not specific enough to explain the phenomenon properly because there are too many exceptions.[61] The radicalization in Europe cannot be attributed to a direct spillover of radicalized Arabs emigrating from the Middle East after 9/11 as not even one of the perpetrators of terrorism in Europe was from a middle eastern country.[62] The context is more complicated than many admit and should not be oversimplified based on false and stereotypical assumptions.

The targeted audiences for recruitment by the jihadists are the young Muslims in Europe. Marginalized, often ignored, and viewed as intruders, though born in Europe, youngsters find comfort in jihadist ideology and are easily seduced to become members of radical groups. According to Tibi, "the Al

---

[58] Shaul Shay, *Islamic Terror and the Balkans* (New Brunswick, 2007), 144.

[59] Ibid., 144.

[60] Olivier Roy, "Islamic Terrorist Radicalization in Europe" in *European Islam Challenges for public policy and society*, ed. Samir Amghar, Amel Boubekeur, and Michael Emerson (Brussels: Centre for European policy studies, 2007), 55.

[61] Ibid., 55.

[62] Ibid., 53.

24

Qaeda global networking is mainly based in the European diaspora of Islam."[63] However, there is a certain level of responsibility from European states as they are pushing young Muslims into temptation by denying opportunities for successful integration in the society. The EU tends to portray itself as the major provider of human rights in the World, unintentionally attracting Islamists to infiltrate in Europe and build a network based on "transnational so-called Islamic welfare institutions."[64]

Muslim communities are using the benefits of the welfare programs provided by the Muslim states, and many times they cannot distinguish if the money is intended for other goals. The radicals' method is to use the common Muslims as a cover for their operations, which make tracking the establishment of dangerous networks very difficult. In that way, they are achieving two goals. First, they can operate under protection of the official welfare programs, and second, they are initiating Islamophobia among the Europeans that later help them convert "moderate" Muslims to radical. Whenever some government official points out that jihadist Islamism is a security threat for Europe, not only will the Muslim community not support him, but often he is accused of Islamophobia.[65] The challenge that European leaders are facing is how to confront radical Islam and at the same time protect the principles of the democracy. Europeans tend to equate political Islam with radical Islam and the traditional outfit and dress code is considered as distasteful and a potential threat.

Europeans occasionally do not want to accept the fact that they reside with Muslims and they share the continent with them. Moreover, the Europeans are the ones that invited immigration from the former colonies during the 1960s an 1970s when a labor force was needed. "The existing Islamic enclaves in Europe, called ''parallel societies,'' indicate that Muslim immigrants are not integrated and are not yet

---

[63] Bassam Tibi, *Political Islam, World Politics and Europe - Democratic Peace and Euro - Islam Versus Global Jihad* (New York: Routledge, 2008), 104.

[64] Ibid., 126.

[65] Ibid., 107.

a part of Europe."[66] Some Europeans countries try to solve the problem of radicalization of the young Muslims through integration policy. In April 2005, the Dutch government identified that education and emancipation of the young Muslims in the society is the only way to protect them from the temptation of the Islamists.[67] Radical Islamists used the lack of participation in political life and social and cultural exclusion to mobilize the unsatisfied youth.[68]

On several occasions, Europeans imams tried to spread "fatwa" among the European Muslims, using radical propaganda and targeting young European Muslims with propaganda videos of jihad from the wars in Muslim world.[69] Many European Muslim authors believe that the integration of the Muslim population in Western European societies failed due to lack of "political participation in European affairs at both national and local levels" in the past 30 years.[70] There are cases when European governments try to export the problem in the Muslim world, by launching "expulsion campaigns against foreign imams to their countries of origin,"[71] instead of preventing radicalization among their young population by integration. One of the solutions is to convince the European Muslims leaders to develop tolerant and open Islam, because as Konrad points out, increased political pressure unintentionally forces European

---

[66] Ibid., 40.

[67] Bernard Godard, "Official Recognition of Islam" in *European Islam Challenges for public policy and society*, ed. Samir Amghar, Amel Boubekeur, and Michael Emerson (Brussels: Centre for European policy studies, 2007), 192.

[68] Amel Boubekeur, "Political Islam in Europe" in *European Islam Challenges for public policy and society*, ed. Samir Amghar, Amel Boubekeur, and Michael Emerson (Brussels: Centre for European policy studies, 2007), 36.

[69] Ibid., 18.

[70] Ibid., 17.

[71] Ibid., 18.

Muslims into faith-led activities.[72]

As a secular and moderate Muslim that accepted the values in Europe while living and working in Germany, Tibi is advocating the term "Euro Islam" as a long-term solution for Europe and its Muslim residents. He clearly wants to make a distinction between "the religion of Islam (that he shares) and Islamism as a political totalitarian ideology represented by a movement based in transnational religion."[73] He vows that if Muslims want to be accepted in Europe, they should accept European secularism and preserve their belief system without disturbing the core values of the Western European way of life.

The concept of Euro Islam represents accepting of European values by Muslim immigrants. The strict concept of shari'a is not compatible with the democratic system, pluralism, and basic human rights accepted as a way of life in Europe: "the Islamization of Europe that Islamists envision – and some do not like to acknowledge – is a threat to European identity and to the civil open society."[74] In this matter, it is not negotiable and Europeans will not tolerate shari'a law. If the Muslims in Europe want to be accepted and accommodated, they must tolerate the natives that are the majority and obey the laws produced in a democratic and secular system, not traditionally inherited, or based on religious belief. Tibi is critical towards fundamental Muslims and ask them to stop resisting European values and accept the native's way of life by preserving their own in a moderate, secular form of Euro-Islam. However, he does not exonerate Europeans of the responsibility to integrate Muslims in their society, saying that in the past twenty years, Europeans accidentally galvanized Muslim fundamentalism by excluding and marginalizing

---

[72] Konrad Pedziwiatr, "Muslims in Europe: Demography and organizations," in *Islam in the European Union, Transnationalism, Youth and the War on Terror*, ed. Yunas Samad and Kasturi Sen, (Oxford University Press 2007), 56.

[73] Bassam Tibi, *Political Islam, World Politics and Europe - Democratic Peace and Euro - Islam Versus Global Jihad* (New York: Routledge, 2008), xii.

[74] Ibid., xiv.

the Muslim immigrants.[75]

The question that Tibi is asking Muslims is if they can modify Islam to become European. In addition, if it is difficult to convince the European born Muslims, how it is possible to secularize the incoming immigrants?[76] It is well known that fundamental Islamic teaching "urges Muslims to migrate in order to spread Islam" (da'wa).[77] How it is possible to secularize Muslims that are migrating with a strong belief to spread their values and not accepting the native ones? The contemporary Muslim clerics are acknowledging that Islam failed to dominate Europe by force, so now they are returning to the peaceful spreading of Islam by "increasing Islamic migration to Europe and creation of Islamic parallel societies as ''enclaves'' emerging throughout Europe."[78]

Still, many Europeans are convinced that Islam is incompatible with a European lifestyle. The concept of secularism and democracy pose a legal barrier to the fundamental Islam. There is official encouragement that "the legal systems of the EU countries have the necessary instruments to deal with and solve most of these problems."[79] However, the truth is that it is very difficult to meet fundamentalist needs without interfering with European legal system. At the end of the day, there are often cynical solutions like denying wearing a headscarf in schools because it is not a standard uniform[80] or decibel limitations to mosques.

So far, the attempt at cultural assimilation of Muslims in Western Europe has seen failed

---

[75] Bassam Tibi, *Political Islam, World Politics and Europe - Democratic Peace and Euro - Islam Versus Global Jihad* (New York: Routledge, 2008), xix.

[76] Ibid., 2.

[77] Ibid., 2.

[78] Ibid., 2.

[79] "Islam in the European Union: What's at stake in the future?" (study requested by the European Parliament's committee on Culture and Education, Brussels, 14 May 2007), 59.

[80] Ibid., 90.

assimilation in France, segregation in Germany, and multiculturalism in the Netherlands and the United Kingdom.[81] Young Muslims born in Europe are failing to integrate into the societies they have been raised and resort to building Islamic ghettoes in the major capitals of Western Europe. Although second or third generation citizens in these countries, they have become resistant to the democratic values over the past twenty years. The question is if this phenomena is connected with the friction between "West and the rest" after the end of the Cold war and the enhanced presence of Western countries in the affairs of Muslim states that lies on the soil of ancient Caliphate.

Islam in the Balkans

Today, some eight million Muslims live in the Balkans,[82] which equates to nearly one-third of the Muslim population in Europe. Muslims in the Balkans live in all Balkan states. After the Ottoman invasion in the fifteenth century, a significant number of the Balkan population converted to Islam. The Ottoman political system offered protection, privilege, and better social position to people if they convert. Dependent on the pressure in different parts of the region, people accepted Islam out of necessity. Still, the majority of the Balkan population preserved their Christian faith.

The Muslims in the Balkans are members of different ethnic groups. They have a greater sense of national identity as they developed through many years since the Ottoman occupation of the Balkans, in contrast with the Muslims in Western Europe who are far more recent immigrants and largely unassimilated coming after the end of the colonialism or labor migration in the past five decades. It is evident that all Muslims in the Balkans share a common form of Islam known as Hanafi Sunni, which

---

[81] Leiken, S. Robert, "Europe's Angry Muslims," *Foreign Affairs,* Vol. 84 Issue 4, (Jul/Aug 2005):120-135.

[82] Xavier Bougarel, "The role of Balkan Muslims in building a European Islam," *European Policy Centre* Issue Paper No. 43, (November 23 2005), 6.

originates from Turkey, considered as a more tolerant and moderate form of Islam.[83]

The communist ideology in the Balkans during the Cold War enforced strict secular states and their national identity dwarfed the Muslim kinship. The Muslims in the urban areas stayed more secularized compared to the Muslims in the rural areas.[84] For example, even two decades after the collapse of Communism, Muslims in the Balkans view wearing the veil "as a symbol of rural life and backwardness."[85] Not until the collapse of communism in the Balkans and the introduction of democracy and pluralism in southeastern Europe, did Balkan Muslims start to recognize its traditional roots.[86] There is a shared opinion among Bosniaks and Albanians that their development as "autonomous political actors goes hand in hand with the politicization of their ethnic identity."[87]

Some Albanian clerics argue that the Islamic religion protected them from cultural assimilation of the dominant Christian Greeks and Serbs.[88] This is not entirely true because some minor Christian nations in the Balkans did not accept Islam and Ottoman protection and still preserved their distinctive cultures today (Macedonians and Montenegrins). Still, this claim sought to explain why Albanian insurgents, whose founders were former communists and thus very secular Muslims, "attempted to instrumentalize Islam for national and political aims."[89]

However, some argue that the fear of Muslim unification in the Balkans is debatable because

---

[83] Risto Karajkov, "The Young and the Old: Radical Islam Takes Root in the Balkans", *Worldpress.org*, May 3, 2006, http://www.worldpress.org/Europe/2335.cfm, (accessed March 10, 2011).

[84] Xavier Bougarel, "The role of Balkan Muslims in building a European Islam," *European Policy Centre* Issue Paper No. 43, (November 23 2005), 7.

[85] Ibid., 11.

[86] Xavier Bougarel, "Islam and politics in the post - communist Balkans" (paper presented for the Socrates Kokkalis Student Workshop : New Approaches to Southeast Europe, Cambridge, February 12-13, 1999), 1.

[87] Ibid., 8.

[88] Ibid., 10.

[89] Ibid., 11.

there is much evidence that the national identity is still stronger than Muslim identity. The Bosnian Muslims and the Kosovo Albanians that immigrate to Western Europe, "jealously preserve their autonomy from the tutelage of their Turkish big brothers."[90] Many Balkan Muslims do not want to be equated with the Turkish population, as it links them with the heritage of the Ottoman rule on the Balkans, which challenges their current secular and modern identity. Compared with the European Muslims, the Muslims in the Balkans "are part of a regional geopolitical context dominated by ethnic and religious nationalism, which in turn gives rise to specific types of political mobilization."[91] Not just the Muslims, but also the Orthodox and Catholic Christians in the Balkans, have always perceived religion as a full package together with the ethnicity, culture, and identity and not the dominant determinator of identity. During the Ottoman rule, Christian nations in the Balkans protected their identity by maintaining their religion, and after the Ottomans left, the minority Muslims did the same.

Although overshadowed by the failure of the Muslim integration in Western Europe, the unification of Muslim populations in the Balkans through growth of political Islam following the Yugoslav wars portrays an important shift of influence of Islam on European soil in the last decade.[92] "In the 1990s, the Balkan Muslim communities not only created their own political parties, but also various reviews and newspapers, cultural associations, charitable societies or intellectual forums."[93] This trend began with the national struggle for independence in Bosnia, where the Bosniak population that was "one of the most secularized of the Balkans"[94] and was willing to accept mujahedeen help in the Bosnian war.

---

[90] Ibid., 6.

[91] Xavier Bougarel, "The role of Balkan Muslims in building a European Islam," *European Policy Centre* Issue Paper No. 43, (November 23 2005), 8.

[92] Xavier Bougarel, "Islam and politics in the post - communist Balkans" (paper presented for the Socrates Kokkalis Student Workshop : New Approaches to Southeast Europe, Cambridge, February 12-13, 1999), 2.

[93] Ibid., 5.

[94] Ibid., 16.

This instrumentalization of Islam for projecting politics became a menace, because the radical Islamists that infiltrated Bosnia as mujahedeen did not fight for Bosnian independence, but for Muslim ideology.

After the collapse of the Soviet Union, the Islamists perceived their victory as a beginning of the global jihad in the name of Islam seeking opportunity anywhere. Mujahedeen victory in Afghanistan initiated radicalization of Islam in the Balkans[95] when former Bosnian president Alija Izetbegovic invited jihadists into the Bosnian war, and called for Umma through the "Islamic declaration."[96] The first Mujahedeen fighters arrived and fought as early as October 1992.[97] They have become part of the Bosnian army and until the end of the war, their number was estimated by some to be in the thousands, although the exact number is difficult to determine. The London Institute for International Strategic Studies estimated that foreign volunteers that served in the Muslim forces in Bosnia numbered as much as 40,000 fighters.[98] Two other forms of assistance provided to Bosnian Muslims from the Muslim countries, were humanitarian aid through Islamic charities, and official military aid. Biased authors claim that all the humanitarian and military aid was aimed at fomenting jihad, although most of it ended as humanitarian aid to the civilian population. Bosnia had a right to obtain allies and it was natural that Muslim countries would help. Whether or not this help was sought as part of global jihad is highly debatable.

However, it is an undeniable fact that many terror organizations, mujahedeen fighters, and other radicals used these channels to infiltrate and fight jihad despite the wishes of the local Bosniaks. Shay provides evidence that the humanitarian and military materials final destination were the jihadist fighters.

---

[95] Shaul Shay, *Islamic Terror and the Balkans* (New Brunswick, 2007), 46.

[96] Ibid., 44.

[97] Ibid., 64.

[98] Ibid., 68.

Even if this is biased assumption, the UN peacekeeping force in the country was supposed to monitor all the help that entered Bosnia. Shay lists a number of other Islamic charities from other countries such as Iran and Kuwait[99] that were legal and well known to UN. It is not fair to simply hold Muslim countries responsible for the radical Islam in Bosnia[100] (even if some governments had such intentions) because everything happened in front of the eyes of Western Europe and the UN peacekeepers.

Although many mujahedeen fighters simply did not have anywhere to go after the Balkan war, some of them truly believed in the "apocalyptic, one-dimensional religious confrontation between Muslims and non-Muslims"[101] on a global scale. War in the Balkans was well timed for organizations like Al Qaida. Terrorist networks used the Bosnian war as an opportunity to get closer to the West. "For Osama bin Laden and other terrorist masterminds, the strategic value of Bosnia lied in its "human resources" capacity for becoming a net exporter of jihad in the never-ending struggle to establish a global caliphate."[102] For radical Islam, "Bosnia represented the seamless continuation of a single holy war, simply the next front in a long war to spread Islam by the sword."[103]

After the Dayton Accords in 1995 and official end of the war in Bosnia, over 1000 mujahedeen stayed in the country and got Bosnian citizenship.[104] The Bosnian president granted them citizenship as a reward for their contribution in the Bosnian Muslim army. Some mujahedeen veterans were already incorporated "in senior positions within the Muslim Bosnian administration, the police, the legal system,

---

[99] Ibid., 6.

[100] Ibid., 51.

[101] Evan Kohlmann, *Al - Qaida's Jihad in Europe - the Afghan - Bosnian Network* (New York, 2004), 28.

[102] Christopher Deliso, *The Coming Balkan Caliphate - The Threat of Radical Islam to Europe and the West* (London, 2007), 6.

[103] Ibid., 6.

[104] Shaul Shay, *Islamic Terror and the Balkans* (New Brunswick, 2007), 69.

and management."[105] Many retired in the villages as permanent residents, married Bosnian wives, and organized their communities using the Wahhabi belief. Later the Bosnian government would find this as a problem as the pressure from the EU will grow to get rid of the former mujahedeen fighters that obviously created a bad image for Bosnia while pursuing EU integration.

According to Kohlmann, the tactical network of Al Qaida proceeded with maintaining the training camps in Bosnia with hundreds of new Muslim volunteers despite the fact that the Bosnian war was almost over.[106] The Dayton Accords were not what the foreign fighters expected because Bosnia did not became an Islamic state as they probably thought they would, but a federation with "the infidels." The agreement stated that the Bosnian government must force out mujahedeen foreign fighters, but to evade this decision, "Izetbegovic's regime issued thousands of Bosnian passports, birth certificates, and other official paperwork."[107] This was done for two reasons, as a reward for the job well done, and for fear that they might be needed if the peace agreement does not work.

After the end of the war, the Muslim countries continued to support Bosnia through charity institutions. According to Shay, this was not only because of simple altruism, because the EU and NATO already took huge responsibility in the reconstruction of Bosnia. Shay primarily points to Saudi Arabia as a bastion of the Wahhabi movement, responsible for exporting "radical Islam concepts,"[108] thus projecting the soft power of Islam through networks of charities and humanitarian and financial aid, and education of Imams. He claims that Saudi Arabia intentionally assisted Bosnian Muslims with a goal of spreading the Wahhabi form of Islam[109] which is more fundamental compared with the moderate

---

[105] Ibid., 69.

[106] Evan Kohlmann, *Al - Qaida's Jihad in Europe - the Afghan - Bosnian Network* (New York, 2004), 140.
[107] Ibid., 163.

[108] Shaul Shay, *Islamic Terror and the Balkans* (New Brunswick, 2007), 47.

[109] Ibid., 49.

Balkan's Islamic ideology spoiled by secularism and communism. Iran's huge medical center in city of Bihac build in June 1996, was also seeking a dominant role in front of the Arab Muslim countries and opportunities for eventual future soft power projection.[110] Shay believes that all these charities, humanitarian and military aid and support from the Muslim countries on the behalf of Muslims in Bosnia are in fact "foundations for the terror infrastructure"[111] in the Balkans emerging right in front of Western eyes.

Many charities from the Muslim countries came to Bosnia with real humanitarian intentions, as it is a fact that the civilian Muslim population in Bosnia needed help. Nevertheless, there was an assessment in 1996 that "nearly one third of the Islamic NGOs in the Balkans have facilitated the activities of Islamic groups that engage in terrorism, including the Egyptian Al Gama`at Al Islamiyya, Palestinian Hamas, and Lebanese Hezbollah."[112] Many of these organizations "directly aided the flow of men and arms to the Arab-Afghan mujahedeen"[113] using the "humanitarian assistance" alibi. Muslim countries continuously blamed the West arguing that they were allowing atrocities toward the Bosnian Muslims, despite those networks so easily being accessed the Balkans in front of the Western presence.

In Bosnia, Muslims, although satisfied that the foreigners came in distress to help them, were not very happy that mujahedeen settled permanently in Bosnian villages. Knowing that they are followers of the Wahhabi style of Islam, and how that image will affect Bosnia if they want to become a member of the EU, Bosnians started to "reclaim their pre-war existences and their unique Euro-Asian heritage."[114] The issue of the departure of the mujahedeen out of Bosnia is still an ongoing problem. Although fear

---

[110] Ibid., 71.

[111] Ibid., 72.

[112] Evan Kohlmann, *Al - Qaida's Jihad in Europe - the Afghan - Bosnian Network* (New York, 2004), 36.

[113] Ibid., 47.

[114] Ibid., 226.

from atrocities perpetrated against the Muslims in Bosnia may open the door for radical Islam, the Bosnian Muslim population does not support it.

It seemed that Western Europe allowed infiltration of fundamental Islam on European soil, at the same time making efforts to integrate Bosnia as a European country. Shay criticizes Western blindness for the growth of Islam in the Balkans arguing that NATO helped Muslims in Kosovo to establish a new country with predominantly Muslim population.[115] However, the reason behind bombing Yugoslavia was never intended to support simply the Muslim cause as Shay claims. It is a false conclusion, because Albanians are quite secular Muslims. The Albanian insurgency has roots from Marxist Leninist ideology in the 1980s. The Albanian agenda has nothing to do with a "clash of civilizations" and Muslims' intention of creating Umma, but unification of all Albanians into a "Greater Albania."

In the eyes of the Muslim World, the same pattern followed in Kosovo similar to Bosnia: Islamic charities from the Muslim countries started to pour in serving as "logistic backup and covered penetration of Islamic activities into the Kosovo arena."[116] The network of charities already existing in Bosnia served as the core for supporting the insurgents in Kosovo.[117] The point is that no matter the cause why the Muslims are fighting, the radical Islamists and in some cases governments of Muslim countries tend to see that Islam is in peril and seek to help any Muslim war effort by any means necessary. Similar to the war in Bosnia, Chechnya and every single conflict where Muslims are involved, the Islamists claimed that the Albanian struggle in the Kosovo war is one more proof for the incompatibility of Islam and infidels. A resolution was passed in October 1998 at a conference of Islamic organizations held in Pakistan "to which the struggle of Muslim Albanians for independence must be regarded as a jihad, and the participants

---

[115] Shaul Shay, *Islamic Terror and the Balkans* (New Brunswick, 2007), 80.

[116] Ibid., 88.

[117] Ibid., 88.

36

called for the Muslim world to fight for the freedom of the occupied Muslim territories."[118]

Deliso blames Western interference in the Balkans (in Bosnia, Kosovo, Macedonia) as partially responsible for the "infestation" of radical Islamists.[119] It is not through deliberate action, but more as a chain of accidental events because of the Western intervention to protect the Muslim population in the Yugoslav wars, that set the conditions for radical Islam.[120] By establishing a firm base in Bosnia, mujahedeen fighters paved the way for exporting jihad outside the Balkans, "toward the primary goal of attacking the global 'infidel' regimes"[121] and "more expansive international holy struggle."[122] Following the Muslim belief that once Islam takes ground it keeps it forever. The coming of the mujahedeen to the Balkans in the 1990s re-opened the chapter from the Balkan history, when Muslims ruled the peninsula for centuries. This more closely resembles Huntington's clash of civilizations.

Building mosques has always been the Islamic method to show the line of conquest. Just in the last decade, hundreds on new mosques were built in the Balkans while the size of the Muslim population did not change. It is very easy to recognize the new Saudi - Wahhabi style mosques in contrast to the traditional Balkan style mosques from the Ottoman architecture, as "The Wahhabists had little tolerance for the traditional aesthetics of Ottoman Islam, to be authentic places of worship, mosques should be white, boxy structures devoid of detail."[123]

Deliso claims that many Western diplomats and journalists deliberately ignored the potential of

---

[118] Ibid., 84.

[119] Christopher Deliso, *The Coming Balkan Caliphate - The Threat of Radical Islam to Europe and the West* (London, 2007), 130.

[120] Ibid., 142.

[121] Evan Kohlmann, *Al - Qaida's Jihad in Europe - the Afghan - Bosnian Network* (New York, 2004), 71.

[122] Ibid., 75.

[123] Christopher Deliso, *The Coming Balkan Caliphate - The Threat of Radical Islam to Europe and the West* (London, 2007), 55.

Bosnia to be a nest for radical Islam, because they "had built large fortunes and careers on protecting this myth of their own making."[124] The Western intention in Bosnia and its mujahedeen residents grew after the 9/11 attack, when it was discovered that there are connections between the Bosnian war and the Hamburg cell: "Mohammad Haydar Zammar, an Al Qaeda operative suspected of having recruited Mohammad Atta into the Hamburg cell, had fought there. Nawaf al Hazmi and Khalid al-Mihdhar, two hijackers on American Airlines Flight 77 that crashed into the Pentagon, were also veterans of the Bosnian jihad, as was Khalid Sheikh Mohammad, the plot's ultimate mastermind."[125] Deliso says it is irrelevant that Balkan Muslims are secular and not interested in Muslim fundamentalism, as long as they receive funding from the Arab World, they are unintentionally opening the door to radicalism.[126] The terrorist networks are using the infrastructure to pursue their agenda nevertheless. Despite the shutdown of many suspected Islamic charities after the 9/11 attacks, many simply changed the names and stayed functional.[127]

Although it is clear that the majority of the Balkan Muslim population is secular, there is increased fear of radicalization imported from outside. The concern that the Balkans is becoming a "breeding ground for the terrorists with easy access to Western Europe"[128] is more real when the alert comes from the Islamic community itself. The threat for Western Europe is potential EU membership of Balkan countries that would allow easy transit to West. It was notable that since the end of the Bosnian war the Wahhabi form of Islam is becoming more popular among the isolated Muslim residents in the

---

[124] Ibid., 4.

[125] Ibid., 12.

[126] Ibid., 158.

[127] Ibid., 160.

[128] Konstantin Testorides, "Radical Islam on rise in Balkans," *The Boston Globe*, September 18, 2010, http://www.boston.com/news/world/europe/articles/2010/09/18/radical_islam_on_rise_in_balkans, (accessed March 3, 2011).

rural areas. Moniquet argues that although radical Islamists favor Western Europe, "the risk of white Al Qaeda members, even females, recruited from the Balkan Muslim communities is a very real one."[129]

When the different Islamic organizations rushed to help their Muslim brethren in the Balkans even adversaries like Saudi Arabia and Iran made "cooperative efforts to aid the Muslim."[130] This indicates that when Islam is at stake, Muslim countries are eager to cooperate even with suspicious and questionable, motivated governments in pursuing the concept of Umma. If this is evident, then it is difficult not to be suspicious that the Muslim world sometimes go blindfolded when radical Islamists and terrorist organizations make use of the legitimate infrastructure to fight their jihad.

That is why many fear that radical Islam is targeting the European continent through the Balkans, using the infrastructure and organizations established during and after the Yugoslav wars. Those are not necessarily intended to serve the terrorist organizations, but they are unintentionally providing the necessary logistic support for promoting radicalism by "establishment of the traditional Islamic way of life, including mosques, cultural centers, and NGO's…to identify potential volunteers for requiting into the ranks of the Islamic jihad."[131] Shay claims that the Balkan instability after the collapse of Yugoslavia created a chaotic environment that "turned this arena into an optimal operational theater for the Islamic terror organizations and Iran."[132] In front of Western European eyes, radical Islam is using the network of Muslim infrastructure in the Balkans as a logistic base for further development of terror organizations. He sees the Balkans as an arena where Islam will attempt to conquer Europe,[133] a process that started

---

[129] Christopher Deliso, *The Coming Balkan Caliphate - The Threat of Radical Islam to Europe and the West* (London, 2007), 173.

[130] Shaul Shay, *Islamic Terror and the Balkans* (New Brunswick, 2007), 184.

[131] Ibid., 143.

[132] Ibid., 201.

[133] Ibid., 202.

centuries ago with Ottoman invasion.

Some believe that it is the intention of Turkey to become a member of EU in order to further challenge Old Europe[134] by importing 70 million more Muslims and thus reestablishing again the lost balance between Muslims and Christians on the old continent. Modern Turks have been secular for the past 90 years, but the memories of the Ottoman Empire, Balkan occupation and the siege of Vienna in the attempt to Islamize Europe has not been forgotten among the Europeans. Turkey is the oldest applicant for membership, constantly adjusting the political system to satisfy European standards, but there is not a sign of hope that its membership will happen soon.

Other authors hold the opposite view on radical Islam in the Balkans. In the past two decades, it is undeniable that radical Islam is attempting to infiltrate the Muslim institutions in the Balkans, but Muslim communities in all states in the Balkans are genuinely concerned for their image and credibility in the eyes of the Europeans and openly resist the ideas coming from the radicals. It is a fact that there has not been serious Islamic violence in The Balkans so far.[135]

According to Pargeter, Bosnian Muslims during the war "became hostage to the ambitions of the old Middle Eastern rivals, Iran and Saudi Arabia, as they sought to extend their influence further into Europe."[136] Ironically, although the West officially took the side of the Bosnian Muslims and NATO attacked Bosnian Serbs, Saudi Islamists claimed that the West was blindfolded to the violence against the Muslims.[137] The atrocities were used to portray that Islam in Europe is in peril and the Muslim world

---

[134] Bassam Tibi, *Political Islam, World Politics and Europe - Democratic Peace and Euro - Islam Versus Global Jihad* (New York: Routledge, 2008), xx.

[135] Risto Karajkov, "The Young and the Old: Radical Islam Takes Root in the Balkans", *Worldpress.org*, May 3, 2006, http://www.worldpress.org/Europe/2335.cfm, (accessed March 10, 2011).

[136] Alison Pargeter, *The New Frontiers of Jihad - Radical Islam in Europe* (Philadelphia: University of Pennsylvania Press, 2008), 40.

[137] Ibid., 40.

should stand up and support the Bosnian Muslims. In return, Saudis expected Bosnian Muslims to accept the Wahhabi way and leave behind "the attachment to nationalism and democracy."[138]

The true target of radical Islamists are the Muslims in Western Europe that started to culturally melt into the countries they live in, not the Muslims in the Balkans that practiced their religion for centuries. The Balkan societies are more traditional than the Western European societies, thus the Muslim belief system was not that much exposed to westernization. The Balkan Muslims have a tradition of moving back and forth in Western Europe as a labor force, migrating to support their families from abroad. At the same time as the Muslims from Africa and Asia migrated as a labor force in Europe, the secular Balkan Islam met the "original" Arab Islam. When fundamental Islam started to pour into Western European mosques, the Balkan Muslim immigrants came in contact with the Wahhabi model and some brought the new style back home.[139] Ironically, despite the fact that the Balkans was the home of Muslims for centuries, radical Islam was imported from The Western Europe.

Bougarel says the Muslim world is not trying to redraw the Balkans geopolitical map at all. The fear of the Muslims intention to create a "Green Axis" that would connect Asia and Western Europe is exaggerated and taken out of context, a product of the fear created by the Muslim terrorists' attacks.[140] The support for the Muslims in the Balkans after the collapse of Communism came from the Muslim countries as a natural legitimate policy of projecting national interests. According to Pargeter, the Bosnian jihad never reached the scale of jihad in Afghanistan. One reason for this was, Bosnia is in the Western

---

[138] Ibid., 41.

[139] Christopher Deliso, *The Coming Balkan Caliphate - The Threat of Radical Islam to Europe and the West* (London, 2007), 75.

[140] Xavier Bougarel, "The role of Balkan Muslims in building a European Islam," *European Policy Centre* Issue Paper No. 43, (November 23 2005), 17.

sphere of interest, and Arab World was reluctant to commercialize jihad like in Afghanistan.[141]

In addition, it was clear that Bosnian Muslims although accepting foreign fighters, they were not willing to abandon their secular way of life and Islamize their country. They still had to consider on European integration after the war was over. The Bosnian jihad was exaggerated and in fact, proof that there was no clear jihadist strategy among the Islamists, and Bosnia became merely a coincidental piece of land for the mujahedeen refugees to take cover.[142] If we take into consideration that these Muslim veterans were homeless and expected some kind of reparation for their deeds in Afghanistan that they did not get, one can assume that one of the reasons for their coming to Bosnia is to seek permanent settlement, not necessarily jihad itself. After all in the Bosnian war there were mercenaries (dogs of war) fighting on all sides, not just Muslim.

Many Islamic communities in the Balkans admit there are attempts of infiltration of Wahhabi scholars and Imams trained in Arab countries, but those incidents are marginal and do not represent a serious threat. The Muslims in the Balkans, with minor exception in Bosnia, still practice Islam as they did in the past, in a moderate and tolerant manner.[143] General opinion is that Wahhabism come into the Balkans "through graduates from foreign universities and Islamic charities."[144] Young Muslims that for a variety of reasons seek education in Arab countries might be influenced by the cultures in those states, but it should not become a stereotype that by definition they vowed radicalism. Exaggerating that Muslims in the Balkans will radicalize so easily and leave their traditional practice of faith should not be encouraged because it could have the opposite effect.

---

[141] Alison Pargeter, *The New Frontiers of Jihad - Radical Islam in Europe* (Philadelphia: University of Pennsylvania Press, 2008), 43.

[142] Ibid., 46.

[143] Risto Karajkov, "The Young and the Old: Radical Islam Takes Root in the Balkans", *Worldpress.org*, May 3, 2006, http://www.worldpress.org/Europe/2335.cfm, (accessed March 10, 2011).

[144] Ibid.

Strategy development and Operational implications

The third hypothesis of this monograph connects the European and the Balkan challenge regarding how to jointly assess and confront the threat of radical Islam. So far, there is no clear, unified European strategy on how to address the potential threat of radical Islam. If there is lack of consensus in defining a valid problem statement, this means it is nearly impossible to develop joint strategy on how to deal with it operationally. The countries of Europe are addressing the problem separately, which is the opposite of the concept of the European vision of cohesive EU. It is obvious that European governments, as a whole, need to jointly define the problem statement for radical Islam soon, and develop a strategy and operational approach to address any real threats posed by radical Islam while simultaneously recognizing secular Islam as a non-threat and even a potential source for combating the more radical elements.

The biggest challenge is the fact that EU is a union of countries, not states like the United States. Each European nation has different national interests and policies, some of them diverging and at odds with one another. Despite the dream of achieving united strategy and operational approach, European countries have issues that will not likely be resolved in near future. When we consider the threat of radical Islam, each country's operational approach will likely be driven by individual countries' assessments of threat. The strategies on how to confront radical Islam varies from a very liberal approach in the United Kingdom, tolerant in the Netherlands, to multicultural approaches of *jus sangunis* (citizenship determined by blood line) in Germany and *jus soli* (birthright citizenship) in France.

The policymakers in European countries must understand that they have to define some common European interests if they want to develop appropriate unified strategy against radical Islam.[145] The

---

[145] Harry R. Yarger, *Strategic Theory for the 21st Century: The Little Book on Big Strategy* (Strategic Studies Institute, February 2006), http://www.strategicstudiesinstitute.army mil/pdffiles/pub641.pdf (accessed July 25, 2011), 50.

strategic objectives of European policy should be concise statements of desired end states. If the policymakers fail to identify or clearly translate the real objectives, "a proposed strategy is fundamentally flawed and cannot be effective."[146] The strategic objective for confronting the spread of radical Islam in Europe should be shaped "by policy guidance, higher strategy, the nature of the strategic environment, and the capabilities and limitations of the instruments of power available."[147]

The vision of Europeans is united Europe without borders. This could facilitate the movement of militant Islamism throughout Europe, as it is essentially one big country. By taking deep roots, radical Islamists networks would patiently wait for the "Europe without boundaries"[148] and an ultimate connection with the radical networks in Western Europe. The integration of all Balkan states in EU would mean unification of the Balkans' and West European Muslims. In such an environment, identification and identity could grow around religion, not nationality. United Europe will bring closer its Muslim population. That is why the vision of a more cohesive union must merge the different national interests into one general European end state. If countries protect their national interests outside of the idea of European interests, it is contradictory to the overall vision. Radical Islamists that attempt to infiltrate Europe see it as a single strategic environment. The Europeans should see it the same way, developing compatible operational approaches.

In the context of the threat from radical Islam, European countries should have the mindset of a single nation state, where "strategy and strategic objectives are derived from the policy consideration of protecting or advancing national interests within the context of the strategic environment as it is, and as it

---

[146] Ibid., 49.

[147] Ibid., 52.

[148] Shaul Shay, *Islamic Terror and the Balkans* (New Brunswick, 2007), 203.

may become."[149] It seems very simple to define European objectives as mere end states: keep Europe safe from radical Islam, keep European Muslims protected from the influence of the radical Islam, and isolate the infiltrated radicals in Europe. The strategic EU objective should be a concrete decision for unified European security in the context of expanding militant Islam and global terror.

Developing strategic concepts or ways is the second element in strategy development. European policymakers must pursue a solution to the problem of radical Islam by clearly defining and explaining how to use the instruments of national power to confront the Islamists in Europe.[150] "Strategic concepts link resources to the objectives by addressing who does what, where, when, and why to explain how an objective will be achieved."[151] Concepts are necessary because they provide basic guidance and directives to the executive elements that work in the streets of Europe.

So far, different European countries have different strategic concepts regarding how to influence the mindset of the Muslim population in the attempt to discourage them from becoming victims of the militant Islam. In many cases, it caused either Islamophobia among Europeans or discouraged the Muslim integration forcing them to protect their identities in the ghettoes. Usually the strategic concepts may cause undesirable second and third order effects in the complex systems that lead to new problems.[152] One of the challenges is to prevent the interception of the Islamists' activities in Europe to be perceived as a "witch hunt." There must be a clear distinction between political Islam and fundamentalism, and more specifically, between the grey line of fundamentalism and its militant form.

Many countries will build their concepts based on their national interest and agendas. Even with a

---

[149] Harry R. Yarger, *Strategic Theory for the 21st Century: The Little Book on Big Strategy* (Strategic Studies Institute, February 2006), http://www.strategicstudiesinstitute.army mil/pdffiles/pub641.pdf (accessed July 25, 2011), 49.

[150] Ibid., 55.

[151] Ibid., 55.

[152] Ibid., 57.

joint definition of the desired ends, there is no guarantee that countries and regions in Europe will agree on the same strategic concepts. In this sense, the Balkans' approach will be much different from the West European approach because of a different environmental frame - the recent ethnic wars where Muslims were involved. A general concept so far was to find ways to integrate the Muslim population into the European culture either through developing Euro Islam in Western Europe or maintaining Balkans' secularism. However, recent announcements from UK, France, and Germany as leaders in Europe, that the idea of multiculturism is a failed project should be a primary concern when planning the strategic concepts.

Additionally, because there is a significant difference between the Muslims in the Balkans and Muslims in West Europe that means there must be different strategic concepts of influencing the Muslim population in Europe. Unified strategy may not be valid in a different environmental framework. This is contradicting the whole idea of Unified European operational approach in solving the problem. One thing is clear, the Balkans is part of Europe, and the problem of radical Islam cannot be partially solved. European policymakers must at least agree on similar ways of integration as a primary concept to make them immune to the influence of radical Islamists.

In the process of developing a strategy against radical Islam, European planners have to agree to devote sufficient "types and levels of resources that are necessary to support the concepts of the strategy."[153] Recourses in strategy are the means by which the concepts will accomplish the objectives. There are tangible and intangible resources, both with issues of their practical employment.[154] Tangible resources are the hardware of the countries, their security forces, technology and equipment, finance and

---

[153] Harry R. Yarger, *Strategic Theory for the 21st Century: The Little Book on Big Strategy* (Strategic Studies Institute, February 2006), http://www.strategicstudiesinstitute.army mil/pdffiles/pub641.pdf (accessed July 25, 2011),60.

[154] Ibid., 61.

infrastructure. European countries, even the Balkans, have enough materiel as effective means to dedicate for internal security.

The challenge of European countries is the intangible resources. These resources are the software of the strategy, like the individual nations' will for European security, dedication to the vision, supportive behavior, accepting radical Islam as a joint European problem and compliance with the decisions made by the majority of Europeans. In contrast to the tangible resources, these are not measurable; they are often volatile and might be problematic for building strategy in an environment like Europe, which is not coherent.[155] Similar to the diametrically opposed approaches about the objectives and concepts, European countries so far had incompatible tangible ways of addressing the problem. "Allocating inadequate resources for a strategic concept is a recipe for disaster, and will cause even greater costs in recovering."[156]

Possible failure in the attempt to integrate the Muslim population in West Europe is the underestimation of the power that Islamic communities have. In the Balkans, out of necessity they are integral part of the solution, considered as a valuable strategic resource to counter the radical Islamists infiltration among them. Many European Muslims are reluctant to respond to Islamists' offer and quietly view their religion more as a cultural symbol of their heritage or simply "follow the path of agnosticism or religious indifference."[157] Radical Islam is attempting to infiltrate and convert their behavior, making them a strategic tangible resource for accomplishing their strategic goals. Europeans should identify that the primary strategic resource to fight radical Islam are the European Muslims themselves, and reconsider why some Islamic communities in the past two decades were pushed aside in isolated ghettoes. "Violent

---

[155] Ibid., 61.

[156] Ibid., 62.

[157] "Islam in the European Union: What's at stake in the future?" (study requested by the European Parliament's committee on Culture and Education, Brussels, 14 May 2007), 7.

Islamic extremists can be defeated only by other Muslims."[158]

Several of the Islamic terrorists that perpetrated the 9/11 attack had been active in Europe before, making the Europeans aware that radical Islam from their backyard exported terror to the United States.[159] The responsibility of the Europeans to have control over these groups became a priority issue for the EU. Europeans supported the United States call for action through NATO, thus opening a new chapter for the alliance, export of security out of the European continent. Although the alliance was not designed to fight terrorism, it became clear that the Western World must stay united in front of the new global threat. However, European countries in contrast of the United States, still see terrorism as a crime problem, not an occasion for war."[160] This additionally can complicate planning considerations of NATO in supporting the United States countering Global Islamic terror.

European planners in NATO were aware of the threat from radical Islam in the Balkans even before 9/11. They had to intervene on several occasions with the infiltrated mujahedeen fighters in Bosnia that caused problems in isolated villages practicing Wahhabi Islam. That was a clear signal for NATO planners that there was indeed presence of Islamists in the Balkans after the Bosnian war. Many Islamists took advantage of the Western concept of democratic and civil rights in Europe, using the Western European system against itself to establish safe havens for radical Islam.[161] However, in the Balkans under the cover of the recent ethno-religious fragile peace, they used the unrestrained Islamic

---

[158] Colin S. Gray, *War, Peace and International Relations* (New York: Routledge, 2007), 262.

[159] Alison Pargeter, *The New Frontiers of Jihad - Radical Islam in Europe* (Philadelphia: University of Pennsylvania Press, 2008), 109.

[160] Leiken, S. Robert, "Europe's Angry Muslims," *Foreign Affairs,* Vol. 84 Issue 4, (Jul/Aug 2005):120-135.

[161] Bassam Tibi, *Political Islam, World Politics and Europe - Democratic Peace and Euro - Islam Versus Global Jihad* (New York: Routledge, 2008), 112.

organizations and charities as infrastructure necessary for their activities.[162]

The operational challenge for European planners is how to support the Balkans' governments to counter radical Islam, knowing that they might pursue their national agenda in the context of never ending Balkan's ethno-religious issues. The fact is that every conflict in the Balkans will end up as religious in the eyes of the Muslim world. Bosnia is proof that Arab countries "viewed Muslim communities in Europe as an extension of the Islamic world and sought to spread their influence among them."[163] Kosovo is proof that the creation of the nation states in the Balkans is not over. While Muslims in EU "never challenge the political institutions - and even less the territorial integrity - of existing nation states, in the Balkans, political parties representing Muslims are constituted on an ethnic basis and make national claims which may go as far as demanding territorial autonomy or outright independence."[164]

According to Shay, the biggest challenge for the Balkan future is complication of the Bosnian scenario. With secession and independence of Kosovo, the Serb Republic in Bosnia may pursue the same path. If it is a legitimate solution for Kosovo Albanians to declare independence, it is possible that Serbs in Bosnia ask for secession also. That would destabilize the Muslim-Croatian federation and foment unrest, based on religion and again viewed from Muslim world as attack on Islam. In addition, it is widely accepted assumption that any more serious conflict in the Balkans where Muslims are involved can lead to intervention from Turkey, which would complicate regional stability and relations with Greece. Shay is offering a solution. He argues that the EU should integrate the "black hole states" as soon as possible and

---

[162] Christopher Deliso, *The Coming Balkan Caliphate - The Threat of Radical Islam to Europe and the West* (London, 2007),147.

[163] Alison Pargeter, *The New Frontiers of Jihad - Radical Islam in Europe* (Philadelphia: University of Pennsylvania Press, 2008), 206.

[164] Xavier Bougarel, "The role of Balkan Muslims in building a European Islam," *European Policy Centre* Issue Paper No. 43, (November 23 2005), 21.

to bring economic benefits on the negotiation table.[165]

If there is no joint security strategy in the EU, should we expect joint strategy on radical Islam in Europe including the Balkan countries' security? The Balkan countries that have a significant Muslim population are not yet EU members. There are many reasons for this, mainly economic, but one of the standards that the EU constantly imposes is the issues with security. Europeans view the Balkans as a potential crisis region in Europe. They perceive the recent Yugoslav wars as pure religious wars, which is one of the misunderstandings among EU policymakers.

At the same time, the Balkans' "experts" often exaggerate the problem with Islam, with the purpose of earning sympathies from the West. It is a pattern established during the Yugoslav wars, but particularly after 9/11 and the global war on terror. Many "experts on terrorism" rose in the Balkans after 9/11, blaming the Muslim co-citizens for instability in the region. There are ambiguous analyses for Bosnia, while some are neglecting the mujahedeen presence saying that the threat is minor, many reports are alerting significant connection of Bosnian networks with the attacks in Europe. The unbiased conclusion is that many times the radical Islam and terrorist activities connected to global networks is a card played in the Balkans by the states to attract international attention in their interethnic policies: "Serbian and Bosnian Serb politicians often make charges of Al Qaeda training camps in Bosnia and Kosovo in an effort to discredit Bosniaks and Albanians."[166]

In future, Muslim states in the Balkans will continue to pursue their European heritage, while preserving their loyalty toward Islam, receiving offered help from the Muslim world. The other Balkan states will pursue their national interests and see Islam as a threat not just for the Balkans, but also for the whole continent of Europe, wondering how the Western Europeans cannot see that. Both will seek EU

---

[165] Shaul Shay, *Islamic Terror and the Balkans* (New Brunswick, 2007), 202.

[166] Steven Woehrel, "Islamic Terrorism and the Balkans," (CRS Report for Congress, July 26, 2005).

and NATO support, first in the name of self-determination, freedom of religion and human rights, and the second in the name of preventing global Islamic terrorism, century's old clash of civilizations and threat for European way of life.

Many non-Muslims in the Balkans believe that Europeans are not willing to integrate the Balkan countries because of the significant Muslim population and the alleged Radical Islam that entered the Balkans. If that were true, it would be a paradox, because the Muslims in the Balkans are more willing to defend their European background from the radical Islamists, than the newcomer-Muslims in the EU. False assumptions regarding the level of threat in the Balkans will result in a false problem statement. The operational implications of misunderstanding the real threat will have impacts on the complete Balkans' integration in EU. Additionally, it will have impact on the EU strategy to stop radical Islam overall.

Leaving the Balkans behind because of the assumption that its integration will bring more Muslims in the Union may have several negative effects. If the EU tries to isolate the Balkans Muslims, the non-Muslims will blame them for the failure of integration. This can disturb already fragile ethno-religious relations, segregating even more the diverse populations. On the other hand, the Balkan Muslims may leave the policy of ethnic identity and unite under the religious element. That would be the desired situation for the Radical Islamists, which are already rooted in many Balkans' mosques.

In the past decade, the Wahhabi influence in the Balkans spread into the urban areas also. The new-trained Imams educated in the Muslim world are trying to occupy as many mosques as possible. In Macedonia, the official Islamic Religious Community is facing a power struggle to sustain the traditional ways and repel the emerging Wahhabi influence.[167] So far, the Islamic Community is aware of the threat and it is opposing the radicalization of its believers. The Islamic Community acknowledged radical Islam

---

[167] Konstantin Testorides, "Radical Islam on rise in Balkans," *The Boston Globe*, September 18, 2010, http://www.boston.com/news/world/europe/articles/2010/09/18/radical_islam_on_rise_in_balkans, (accessed March 3, 2011).

as a destructive stream that can only damage the image of the Muslim population (predominantly Albanian). There was an actual official request to the government, EU, and United States to help protect the Islamic community from the radicals, after takeover of five mosques in the country's capital.[168]

Therefore, blaming the Balkan Muslims for failure of accepting the European culture is the worst anchor bias that the Balkans' governments can fall to. The Muslims in the Balkans are Europeans in culture and they should not be pushed away toward isolation where they could be vulnerable to radicalization. The secular Balkan Muslims has potential to merge with the concept of European Islam, only if EU shows bigger interest in the Balkans considering the issue of countering the radical Islam.

On the other hand, Western Europeans should reconsider their operational approach in their own backyard. The EU should be more concerned with the Muslim ghettoes in their capitals and the attempt to find joint strategy to integrate their Muslims, because the latest concepts failed. Instead of marking the Balkans as breeding ground for Radical Islam and terrorism, European planners should acknowledge that the real breeding grounds are the ghettoes in the capitals of Western Europe.

Even if the Balkans does occasionally accommodate radicals that hide among the Balkans' Muslim communities, their final destination is always the West. That is why the Balkans must be part of the solution and maybe a model how to divert European Muslims from the temptation of Islamists. Europeans have always been afraid of the so-called balkanization of Europe. However, the balkanization of European Muslims may be the real solution to stop islamization of Europe.

---

[168] "Macedonia: Moderate Muslims seek help against sect", *The Boston Globe*, (September 20, 2010), http://www.boston.com/news/world/europe/articles/2010/09/20/macedonia_moderate_muslims_seek_he p_against_sect/, (accessed April 26, 2011).

CHAPTER 5
CONCLUSIONS AND RECOMMENDATIONS

General conclusions

In the last two decades, Islamic culture showed patterns of increased incompatibility with Western values. The rise of the radical and militant Islam everywhere in the World found a firm base among the Islamic fundamentalists boosted from the misinterpreted ideology of political Islam. The emergence of radical Islam in the heart of Western society is unquestionably a political threat to the West in general.

Muslims in Western Europe, although second and third generation immigrants, are becoming more and more reluctant to accept the European ways of life and tend to return to their traditional beliefs that are fundamentally different from the European concept of human and citizen rights embedded in democratic society. The radical Islamists developed networks in Europe, planned, and conducted terrorist attacks, and represent a major threat for the European security in future.

This monograph reevaluated the intensity of radical Islam in the Balkans compared with the same problem that Western Europe is facing. Claims that the Balkans is the exclusive breeding ground for radical Islam in Europe are shifting the focus from the emerging Western European radical networks. The bottom line is that the Balkans is part of Europe, it has always been part of Europe, and everything that happens in the Balkans will have an impact on European security as a whole.

Preventing radical Islam in the Balkans is a complex problem for Europe because of the ghosts of the latest ethno-nationalist wars that grew into religious conflicts. Wars in former Yugoslavia were fought based on the idea of self-governance, nation building, independence, and self-determination. Balkans' Muslim population in the eyes of the Muslim community around the World became the victim of the Christian dominated population. This was a paradox because the West had de facto helped, supported, and protected the Balkan Muslims in all cases, culminating with military intervention to protect them. Europeans consciously permitted Islamic organizations to infiltrate in the Balkans. While many had true humanitarian goals, it was a package that went hand in hand with radical networks seeking their own agenda.

What Europe did not expect was leftover radical Islamists, mujahedeen veterans, indoctrinated imams, and pockets of networks connected with the international Islamic terrorist groups. In the attempt to enforce permanent peace on the Balkans, Western Europeans injected the idea of multiculture tolerance, which turns out to be a failed project in their own backyard. Today the disappointment of multiculturism in Europe is discouraging for the Balkan nations that accepted the model. The results are double standards toward Muslim culture, perceived as good old Western European cynicism, "do what I tell you, do not do what I do."

For now, it seems that Western Europe is ignoring the Balkans' warnings on the threat from radical Islam. Either because Europeans are aware that they have "some" responsibility, and they finally understand the historical and cultural complexity of the Balkans, or they simply are facing the same problem on a larger scale in their countries as well and set themselves as priority. What Europe must understand is that everything that happens in the Balkans will have an impact on them as well. The borders do not matter anymore and the Balkan quagmire cannot be isolated anymore.

Specific conclusions

Just because radical Islam in the Balkans is temporarily concealed, does not means it is not a significant threat. The connections of several members in the international terrorist networks can be tracked through the Balkans, including some Al Qaeda cells responsible for the attacks in Europe after 9/11. So far, the radical Islamists have not directly targeted the Balkans' countries, but they have used them as logistic base for their operations. European security in the future will depend on Balkan stability.

However, when dealing with warnings from the radicalization of the Muslim population,

54

Europe is very cautious. Policymakers are concerned about second and third order effects in the Balkans. The fragile peace in the multiethnic environment can be easily disturbed if they trigger non-Muslim majority in the Balkans to become more decisive in restricting the fundamentalist Muslims. In any further analysis evaluating the threat of radical Islam in the Balkans, European policymakers and planers must be aware of the ambiguous and complex nationalistic policies in the Balkans.

Muslims will always seek support and recognition from the West and portray themselves as victims, at the same time using any support offered from their Muslim kin anywhere in the world. At the same time, non-Muslims will exaggerate the threat from Islam as a continuous, epic battle between civilizations. Some will claim that they are the actual defenders of Western civilization. Sitting on the edge of the civilized world, as martyrs against the Islamic threat, they seek not just support, but gratitude from the west for the sacrifice they make!

Despite the latest concerns on the issue, there is no sign of consistent Western European, Balkans, or joint strategy on combating radical Islam. On the national level, each country has its own measures how to accommodate, integrate, or assimilate Muslims in the European culture. Some use drastic measures that work as a temporary solution, but the problem of spreading Islamic ways in Western Europe is deliberately underestimated and ignored. On the other side, the Balkan governments more often demonstrate concerns, but any serious action against radicals might be interpreted as a move against the Muslims and ignite ethno-religious conflict. Radicals successfully hide under the protection of Islam in general. More and more mosques are built every day in Bosnia, Kosovo, and Macedonia influenced by Wahhabism, in front of the eyes of the EU and NATO.

Indoctrinated Imams trained in the Muslim countries in the past two decades promoted and encouraged Islamic laws among young Muslims in Europe, which is clearly incompatible and unacceptable in democratic societies. In the past decade, the influence of the fundamental Islam is visible and transparent in the streets. Thus, the Islamic communities in the Balkans and Western

55

Europe are the center of gravity for both, radical Islamists and the European security. If the religious leaders throughout Islamic communities in Europe are not recognized as crucial actors for integration of Muslims into European culture, they will be pushed away from European ways.

European governments need to support and influence the Islamic communities' leaders through strategic communication on the national and European level to resist the misinterpreted views of Islam that radicals imported in the past decades. Eventually the Muslim population will become a victim of radical Islam directly by the radicals or indirectly by the Europeans as they will lose credibility and will became unwanted. Any further support to radical Islam even by individuals will enhance the already existing Islamophobia among Europeans.

Recommendations

Radical Islamists in the Balkans are making a stronghold and developing networks. If European operational planners neglect these facts, it will be a serious threat for European security in the near future. Balkan governments are not willing to address the issue more aggressively, first because Balkan countries are not under direct threat yet, and second, some of them lost their sovereignty over making such serious decisions without blessings from Western Europe. Western Europeans are partially responsible for permitting or not preventing the presence of radical Islamists in the Balkans but should get over it and start encouraging Balkan governments to act as soon as possible.

European countries must establish a joint and decisive strategic concept for preventing radicalization of its Muslim population, including the Balkan countries. Balkan security depends on Western European support and it has to become an integrated part of the overall European strategy to intercept radicalization. If European countries intend to truly unite, they must define at least some joint strategic objectives, in the sphere of defense policies, above their national policies. Even among those countries that are not part of the EU, there must be at least joint rules of engagements, clearly defined policies and measures how to treat radical Islamists and sharing of crucial intelligence to track them.

In this fight, the Muslim population is the center of gravity. Europeans must influence and educate European Muslims through strategic communication that the biggest enemy of Islam in Europe is the radical Islam itself. One possible solution is acceptance of the proposed Euro-Islam, which is a balance between practicing Islam and tolerating and respecting the native European culture and laws. The leaders of the Islamic communities are the key for convincing the Muslims not to accept the misinterpreted version of Islam, which vows for jihad and violence against non-Muslims. Indoctrinated Imams should be observed and hate speeches or messages that call for violence should be considered and treated as open hostility.

Radical Islam successfully targeted misplaced European multiculturism in the past two decades, making Europeans question the concept. Their objective was to ignite Islamophobia among Europeans and use that for justifying their struggle for rise of fundamental Islamic ways. Oddly, the level of Islamophobia in the Balkans is significantly lower despite the latest ethno-religious wars. One of the European strategic objectives should be the prevention of Islamophobia among Western Europeans in particular and reconsidering the methods regarding how to achieve multiculturism. Abolishing the whole idea as false is what radicals want.

Ideally, the European policymakers should establish unified European strategy, giving operational planers concrete base to translate the strategic guidance into tactical actions that would accomplish the desired end state. A detailed environmental frame should depict the patterns of spreading radical Islam across Europe, especially the connection between the West Europe and the Balkans. The key to success is defining an ultimate problem statement on radical Islam in Europe that will help synchronize the efforts of all European planners. In that way, there will not be divergence in the operational approaches and the successes in different countries will have cumulative effect toward the ultimate desired end state.

Until this happen, the best thing to do is to adjust and synchronize the tactical successes in countering radical Islam to fit in the general strategic context through regional cooperation.

The operational planners are left to integrate their ends, ways and means using the framework of their own existing national interests and doctrine. This is not a permanent solution, because the vision is EU and rise of European identity above the national. The question is that even if this somehow happens in future, what religious factors will challenge the old European culture? Ultimately, people are loyal to their faith first. There are many examples in the World that even among the homogenous ethnic groups, religion to some point becomes predominant mark, and eventually a source of identity and recognition above the national. Does this mean that further unification of Europe will also unite its Muslim population beyond their national origins? If so, radical Islam will be a threat to Europe as long as it exists as an idea.

APPENDIX

Definitions

Political Islam: Political Islam as a phenomena appeared in the 1980s, after successful Iranian revolution year earlier, and spurring of jihad with Soviet invasion in Afghanistan.[169] It offered hope to those Muslims that craved for returning of the power of Islam denied by the Western powers through their colonialism.

The idea of political Islam began as a response to colonialism and the establishment of the Muslim Brotherhood movement in 1928.[170] The idea to unite all Muslims under one global caliphate and return to the root of the religion was meant to solve the social problems that Muslim believers faced when introduced with westernization.[171] Only through fundamental Islam, which is original and pure, Muslims could achieve unity that is shaken by the interaction with the West through globalization and technology.

Fundamentalism: Fundamentalists refer back to the sources of the religion[172] and it is not necessary violent like radicalism. "Fundamentalism is a religious process that attempts to resist the melting-pot model of secularism, political tolerance, and religious pluralism. Fundamentalism resists the separation of religion and politics, whereby religion is confined to the private

---

[169] Alison Pargeter, *The New Frontiers of Jihad - Radical Islam in Europe* (Philadelphia: University of Pennsylvania Press, 2008), 4.

[170] Ibid., 7.

[171] Ibid., 7.

[172] Jocelyne Ceasari, "The Hybrid and Globalized Islam of Western Europe" in *Islam in the European Union, Transnationalism, Youth and the War on Terror*, ed. Yunas Samad and Kasturi Sen, (Oxford University Press, 2007), 112.

sphere."[173] Globalization tends to disrupt the values and traditions not just in Islam, but also in any other religion, and people respond by returning to their fundamental beliefs as a form of resistance.[174]

Bryan is explaining the fundamentalists' motives that the Idea behind fundamentalism is that "traditional Islam is seen as a compromised form of religious belief and practice that is subordinate to the Western secular influence."[175] While Muslim scholars are seeing this as a reformist movement, which is not necessarily encouraging militancy, for the West it is "attempted to radicalize Islam in the name of its fundamental roots,"[176] generating open rejections towards the Western values and way of life.

Islamism: The terms "Islamism" and "Islamist" are used in the Western societies to describe "radical, militantly ideological versions of Islam, as interpreted by the practitioners and in which violent actions such as terrorism, suicide bombings or revolutions are explicitly advocated, practiced and justified using religious terminology."[177]

For decades, Saudi Arabia is projecting its power by exporting its Wahhabi style of Islam, creating a worldwide network of "humanitarian organizations, educational institutions, cultural centers, orphanages, banks, businesses, and more, all serving the purpose of expanding

---

[173] Bryan Turner, "Orientalism and otherness" in *Islam in the European Union, Transnationalism, Youth and the War on Terror*, ed. Yunas Samad and Kasturi Sen, (Oxford University Press 2007), 63.

[174] Ibid., 63.

[175] Ibid., 64.

[176] Ibid., 64.

[177] Caroline Cox and John Marks, *The 'West', Islam and Islamism - Is Ideological Islam Compatible with Liberal Democracy?,* (London: Institute for the Study of Civil Society, 2003), 6.

the Saudi style of Islam."[178]

Militant and Radical Islam: The generally accepted explanation by the radical Islamists is that the Western world colonized the Muslim world because the Muslims forgot about the principle on which Islam was established, by use of sword. When Muslims used force, they had their Caliphate. Jihadists believe that only through struggle, jihad; they can stop the Western influence that is incompatible with their belief system.

Many authors connect the birth of militant Islam with the fall of communism and end of Cold War. However, Bryan says that Cold war just temporarily interrupted the continuous incompatibility between religions that always existed, "the historical division between the civilizations of the West and the Islamic world."[179]

Jihad: The term jihad is used by Muslims to describe a struggle for the Islamic way of life. There are more interpretations, used by moderates and fundamentalists, but the one perceived by the West is the violent Holy War of the Muslims against non-Muslims.[180]

According to Shay, the jihad organizations are building their doctrine around the concept of unification of all Muslim believers worldwide called Umma.[181] The problem begins with the fact that not all the world countries have majority of Muslim population. There are countries controlled by Islam (Dar al Islam) and countries controlled by infidels (Dar al Harb).[182] The

---

[178]Christopher Deliso, *The Coming Balkan Caliphate - The Threat of Radical Islam to Europe and the West* (London, 2007), 16.

[179] Bryan Turner, "Orientalism and otherness" in *Islam in the European Union, Transnationalism, Youth and the War on Terror*, ed. Yunas Samad and Kasturi Sen, (Oxford University Press 2007), 64.

[180] Caroline Cox and John Marks, *The 'West', Islam and Islamism - Is Ideological Islam Compatible with Liberal Democracy?,* (London: Institute for the Study of Civil Society, 2003), 32.

[181] Shaul Shay, *Islamic Terror and the Balkans* (New Brunswick, 2007), 3.

[182] Ibid., 3.

instruments to achieve Umma are the jihad, which tends to achieve its aims through any means necessary including violence, and the Dawa, which is peaceful spreading of Islam through education and preaching.[183]

Global terror: "In the past two decades… a form of global Islam developed among Diaspora communities that develop solidarity beyond the boundaries of nation and culture, often labeled as transnational networks."[184]

The Afghanistan factor[185] is often viewed as the true establishing of radical Islam and jihad. It is a paradox why Palestinian question never resulted with call for holy war among the Muslim World, while Soviet invasion in Afghanistan united the Muslims like never before.[186] From many Muslim countries, either with secular regimes or monarchies, mujahedeen poured in Afghanistan to fight for Islam. For the first time, "the coming together of Islamists from across the Muslim world brought a sense of shared purpose."[187] It resulted with the birth of Muslim identity that will unite Mujahidin with Bosnian and Chechnya Muslims a decade later.

Although the West, the United States in particular helped the Afghan insurgents defeat the Soviets[188], at the end of the war somehow the Islamists were convinced that they did it because of their faith. From their point of view, victory was achieved because they returned to the fundamentals and jihad as a method of defending Islam. In addition, if they could defeat the

---

[183] Ibid., 3.

[184] Jocelyne Ceasari, "The Hybrid and Globalized Islam of Western Europe" in *Islam in the European Union, Transnationalism, Youth and the War on Terror*, ed. Yunas Samad and Kasturi Sen, (Oxford University Press, 2007), 111.

[185] Alison Pargeter, *The New Frontiers of Jihad - Radical Islam in Europe* (Philadelphia: University of Pennsylvania Press, 2008), 11.

[186] Ibid., 11.

[187] Ibid., 13.

[188] Ibid., 13.

Soviet War machinery, they could bring down any Western power. Unaware that their struggle was a part of a bigger picture (the Cold War),[189] the mujahedeen drew wrong conclusions, and their victory boosted the ideology that gave birth to Al Qaida.

Islamophobia: Islamophobia is a fear in the Western societies from Islam, caused by the recent terrorist activities waged by radical Islamists. "Irrational fear does not make distinctions and therefore a hostile response to Islamist terrorism can quickly spread to hostility to all Muslims."[190]

The fear from Islam in general, but more specific the violent struggle of the radical Islamists, originates from the aim of jihad. The Koran clearly stresses the purpose of jihad, "to establish Islamic authority over the whole world."[191] This makes Islamophobia, although caused by irrational fear, a rational and logical response. The expression "West against the rest" is merely response to the "Islam against the rest," an ideology old as the Muslim religion itself.

---

[189] Ibid., 13.

[190] Caroline Cox and John Marks, *The 'West', Islam and Islamism - Is Ideological Islam Compatible with Liberal Democracy?*, (London: Institute for the Study of Civil Society, 2003), 7.

[191] Ibid., 34.

BIBLIOGRAPHY

Books

Amghar Samir, Boubekeur Amel, and Emerson Michael. *European Islam Challenges for Public Policy and Society*. Brussels: Centre for European policy studies, 2007.

Bawer, Bruce. *While Europe Slept: How Radical Islam is Destroying the West from Within*. New York: Broadway books, 2006.

Boubekeur, Amel. "Political Islam in Europe." In *"European Islam Challenges for Public Policy and Society*, edited by Samir Amghar, Amel Boubekeur, and Michael Emerson, 14-38. Brussels: Centre for European policy studies, 2007.

Ceasari, Jocelyne. "The Hybrid and Globalized Islam of Western Europe." In *Islam in the European Union, Transnationalism, Youth and the War on Terror*, edited by Yunas Samad and Kasturi Sen. Oxford University Press, 2007.

Choudhury, Tufyal. "Muslims and Discrimination." In *European Islam Challenges for Public Policy and Society*, edited by Samir Amghar, Amel Boubekeur, and Michael Emerson, 77-107. Brussels: Centre for European policy studies, 2007.

Cox, Caroline, and Marks John. *The 'West', Islam and Islamism - Is Ideological Islam Compatible with Liberal Democracy?* London: Institute for the Study of Civil Society, 2003.

Deliso, Christopher. *The Coming Balkan Caliphate - The Threat of Radical Islam to Europe and the West*. London, 2007.

Godard, Bernard. "Official Recognition of Islam." In *European Islam Challenges for Public Policy and Society*, edited by Samir Amghar, Amel Boubekeur, and Michael Emerson, 183-204. Brussels: Centre for European policy studies, 2007.

Gray, Colin, S. *War, Peace and International Relations*. New York: Routledge, 2007.

Juergensmeyer, Mark. *Terror in the Mind of God: the Global Rise of Religious Violence*. Los Angeles: University of California Press, 2000.

Kohlmann, Evan. *Al-Qaida's Jihad in Europe - the Afghan - Bosnian Network*. New York, 2004.

Pargeter, Alison. *The New Frontiers of Jihad - Radical Islam in Europe*. Philadelphia: University of Pennsylvania Press, 2008.

Pedziwiatr, Konrad. "Muslims in Europe: Demography and organizations." In *Islam in the European Union, Transnationalism, Youth and the War on Terror*, edited by Yunas Samad and Kasturi Sen. Oxford University Press, 2007.

Roy, Olivier. "Islamic Terrorist Radicalization in Europe." In *European Islam Challenges for Public Policy and Society*, edited by Samir Amghar, Amel Boubekeur, and Michael Emerson, 52-62. Brussels: Centre for European policy studies, 2007.

Shay, Shaul. *Islamic Terror and the Balkans*. New Brunswick, 2007.

Tibi, Bassam. *Political Islam, World Politics and Europe - Democratic Peace and Euro - Islam Versus Global Jihad*. New York: Routledge, 2008.

Turner, Bryan. "Orientalism and otherness." In *Islam in the European Union, Transnationalism, Youth and the War on Terror*, edited by Yunas Samad and Kasturi Sen. Oxford University Press, 2007.

Yarger, Harry R. *Strategic Theory for the 21st Century: The Little Book on Big Strategy*. Strategic Studies Institute, 2006. http://www.strategicstudiesinstitute.army.mil/pdffiles/pub641.pdf (accessed July 25, 2011).

Periodicals

———. "Islam in the European Union: What's at stake in the future?" Study requested by the European Parliament's committee on Culture and Education, Brussels, 14 May 2007.

———. "Macedonia: Moderate Muslims seek help against sect." *The Boston Globe*, September 20, 2010, http://www.boston.com/news/world/europe/articles/2010/09/20/ macedonia_ moderate_muslims_seek_he p_against_sect/, (accessed April 26, 2011).

Bougarel, Xavier. "Islam and politics in the post - communist Balkans." Paper presented for the Socrates Kokkalis Student Workshop: New Approaches to Southeast Europe, Cambridge, February 12-13, 1999.

Bougarel, Xavier. "The role of Balkan Muslims in building a European Islam." *European Policy Centre* Issue Paper No. 43 (2005).

Karajkov, Risto. "The Young and the Old: Radical Islam Takes Root in the Balkans." *Worldpress.org*. May 3, 2006, http://www.worldpress.org/Europe/2335.cfm (accessed March 10, 2011).

Robert, Leiken, S. "Europe's Angry Muslims." *Foreign Affairs,* Vol. 84 Issue 4 (2005): 120-135.

Testorides, Konstantin. "Radical Islam on rise in Balkans." *The Boston Globe*, September 18, 2010, http://www.boston.com/news/world/europe/articles/2010/09/18/radical_islam_on _rise_in_balkans, (accessed March 3, 2011).

Woehrel, Steven. "Islamic Terrorism and the Balkans." CRS Report for Congress, July 26, 2005.